# TERMINOLOGY:
# A PRACTICAL APPROACH

Robert Dubuc

# TERMINOLOGY: A PRACTICAL APPROACH

## Adapted by Elaine Kennedy

with contributions by:

Catherine A. Bowman
Andy Lauriston
Shirley Ledrew

linguatech
éditeur inc.

© 1997 Linguatech éditeur inc.
P.O. Box 92012, Place Portobello
Brossard, Québec J4W 3K8

Registration: fourth quarter of 1997
Bibliothèque nationale du Québec
Canada National Library

All rights reserved. No part of this publication may be reproduced or transmitted in any form or by any means without permission in writing from the publisher.

*Editor:* Shelley Tepperman
*Proofreader:* Lucie Dubuc
*Desktop publisher:* Madeleine Bouvier
*Cover design:* Luc Bouchard and Luis Collazo

**Canadian Cataloguing in Publication Data**

Dubuc, Robert, 1930-
    Terminology: A Practical Approach

Includes bibliographical references and index.
ISBN 2-920342-30-4

    1. Terms and phrases. 2. French Language—Terms and phrases.
I. Kennedy, Elaine, 1954- II. Linguatech (Firm) III. Title.

P305.D82 1997          404'.4          C97-900733-X

*This adaptation is dedicated to Andrew.*

# FOREWORD

*Terminology: A Practical Approach* is intended primarily for students of terminology and translation. However, some chapters—TERM AND CONCEPT, DEFINITIONS IN TERMINOLOGY, SYNONYMY, TERM FORMATION and STANDARDIZATION—may well be of interest to students of technical writing and special subject fields.

This book takes a practical approach to terminology: it treats special language as living language used by people in real-life situations to communicate with one another, and not as a system artificially engineered to meet an ideal. It takes into account the complex weave of factors that can influence the appropriate choice of expression: individual speakers, their place in society, the circumstances under which they communicate, the topic they discuss. It describes natural language in all its diversity and disorder, and the challenges inherent in studying it: the differing perspectives of different languages, the pros and cons of synonyms, the confusion created by polysemous terms within a subject field, the difficulty of keeping step with continually evolving meanings and keeping pace with the proliferation of new terms.

This work is practical not only in the way it treats the vocabulary specific to special languages, but also in the approach it takes to terminological research. After defining terminology as we know it today, establishing it as an independent discipline, and laying down the fundamental principles that govern the practice, the book guides the reader through the stages of term and subject-field research, outlining methods of terminological analysis and parameters for recording terminological data. It points up the importance of using original-language documentation, delves into the role of standardization in English terminology, and discusses the use of new computerized applications in the field.

The practical sections are punctuated by more theoretical sections, which examine the nature of the relationship between term and concept, describe time-honored methods of definition, provide a typology of synonyms, and define the processes of term formation in modern English.

This English version of Robert Dubuc's *Manuel pratique de terminologie* is very much an adaptation. There are two main reasons for this. First, the use of original-language documentation is a fundamental principle in terminology, so a textbook on the subject could hardly be a translation. Second, many aspects of terminological work are different in English, including the basic need for terminology, the reasons for and characteristics of term creation, and the means and objectives of standardization.

Some of the chapters which discuss strictly practical material, including Chapters 5 and 6 on term and subject-field research, have been adapted on the basis of my experience as a practitioner. Most of Chapter 14 on standardization has been made from whole cloth by Cathy Bowman on the basis of her experience and because standardization is so different in English. Most of the other chapters have been researched in English-language sources—when possible—published primarily in the United States and Great Britain, and included in the bibliographies. All of the chapters cover, by and large, the same material as the original French, but the ideas have been organized and discussed as they are presented and treated in English sources.

This work has been a long time in the making, mostly because of the difficulty in reconciling the imperatives of professional practice and academic pursuits. Its publication would not have been possible without the direct or indirect contribution of many people. I owe a debt of gratitude, first and foremost, to Monsieur Dubuc, for the privileged opportunity to study under him, work under his guidance and finally adapt his work. Sincere thanks to Nada Kerpan for exposure to impeccable standards of professional practice. And many thanks to my respected colleagues and lay readers, Marcia Barr and Mary Plaice, and my terminologist readers, Cathy Bowman and Andy Lauriston.

Elaine Kennedy

# TABLE OF CONTENTS

FOREWORD .................................................................................. IX

**CHAPTER 1**
**WHAT IS TERMINOLOGY?** ......................................................... 1
1.0 Introduction ............................................................................ 1
1.1 Beginnings of Modern Terminology ................................... 1
1.2 Definition of Terminology .................................................... 4
1.3 Conclusion ............................................................................ 12
BIBLIOGRAPHY ............................................................................ 13
EXERCISES .................................................................................... 14

**CHAPTER 2**
**THE SITUATION IN TERMINOLOGY** ..................................... 15
2.0 Introduction .......................................................................... 15
2.1 Situation and Living Language .......................................... 16
2.2 Situation and View of Reality ............................................. 16
2.3 Comparative Terminology .................................................. 17
2.4 Situation and Usage ............................................................. 17
2.5 Situation and Users .............................................................. 17
2.6 Situation and Work Method ............................................... 18
2.7 Situation and Standardization ............................................ 19
BIBLIOGRAPHY ............................................................................ 21
EXERCISES .................................................................................... 22

**CHAPTER 3 (Shirley Ledrew)**
**TERMINOLOGY, SEMANTICS AND LEXICOGRAPHY** ........ 23
3.0 Introduction .......................................................................... 23
3.1 Terminology and Semantics ............................................... 23
3.2 Terminology and Lexicography ......................................... 29
BIBLIOGRAPHY ............................................................................ 35
EXERCISES .................................................................................... 35

**CHAPTER 4**
**TERM AND CONCEPT** .............................................................. 37
4.0 Introduction .......................................................................... 37
4.1 Signifier and Signified ......................................................... 37
4.2 What is a Term? .................................................................... 38
4.3 Concept .................................................................................. 39
4.4 Specificity to Subject Field .................................................. 39
4.5 Object ..................................................................................... 40
4.6 Relationship between Term and Concept ......................... 41
4.7 Classification of Concepts ................................................... 44
4.8 Conclusion ............................................................................ 45

BIBLIOGRAPHY ................................................................................. 45
EXERCISES ........................................................................................ 46

## CHAPTER 5

**TERM RESEARCH** .......................................................................... 47
5.0   Introduction ............................................................................ 47
5.1   Advantages of Term Research ............................................. 47
5.2   Steps in Term Research ......................................................... 48
5.3   Why Consult General Works, then Specialized? ............... 51
BIBLIOGRAPHY ................................................................................. 52
EXERCISES ........................................................................................ 52

## CHAPTER 6

**SUBJECT-FIELD RESEARCH** ........................................................ 55
6.0   Introduction ............................................................................ 55
6.1   Stages of Subject-Field Research ......................................... 55
6.2   Conclusion .............................................................................. 61
EXERCISE ........................................................................................... 61

## CHAPTER 7

**TERMINOLOGICAL ANALYSIS** .................................................. 67
7.0   Introduction ............................................................................ 67
7.1   Identification of Terms ......................................................... 67
7.2   Contextual Analysis .............................................................. 71
7.3   Conclusion .............................................................................. 73
EXERCISES ........................................................................................ 73

## CHAPTER 8

**SAMPLE TERMINOLOGICAL ANALYSIS** .................................. 75
8.0   Introduction ............................................................................ 75
8.1   Detection of Terms ................................................................ 76
8.2   Selection of Contexts ............................................................ 79

## CHAPTER 9

**COMPARATIVE TERMINOLOGY** ............................................... 85
9.0   Introduction ............................................................................ 85
9.1   Full Equivalence .................................................................... 85
9.2   Partial Equivalence ................................................................ 86
9.3   Usage Labels .......................................................................... 87
9.4   Limitations of Partial Equivalence ...................................... 90
9.5   Textual Match: The Key to Determining Equivalence of Concepts .............................................................................. 90
9.6   Conclusion .............................................................................. 92
EXERCISES ........................................................................................ 92

## CHAPTER 10
**TERMINOLOGY RECORDS** ............ 93
10.0 Introduction ............ 93
10.1 Definition of Terminology Record ............ 93
10.2 Format ............ 93
10.3 Content ............ 94
10.4 Processing Terminology Records ............ 99
10.5 Conclusion ............ 106
APPENDIX ............ 107
EXERCISES ............ 107

## CHAPTER 11
**DEFINITIONS IN TERMINOLOGY** ............ 109
11.0 Introduction ............ 109
11.1 Rules of Definition ............ 109
11.2 Methods of Definition ............ 111
11.3 Construction of Definitions ............ 113
11.4 Good Defining Practices ............ 115
11.5 Information for a Definition ............ 116
11.6 Conclusion ............ 117
BIBLIOGRAPHY ............ 118
EXERCISES ............ 119

## CHAPTER 12
**SYNONYMY** ............ 121
12.0 Typology of Synonyms ............ 121
12.1 Establishing Synonymy ............ 123
12.2 Studies of Synonyms ............ 125
12.3 Short Sample Studies ............ 126
12.4 Conclusion ............ 129
BIBLIOGRAPHY ............ 130
EXERCISES ............ 130

## CHAPTER 13
**TERM FORMATION** ............ 131
13.0 Introduction ............ 131
13.1 Characteristics of Contemporary English Term Formation ............ 131
13.2 Reasons for Creating Terms ............ 133
13.3 Processes of English Term Formation ............ 134
13.4 General Rules of Term Formation ............ 144
13.5 Who Forms Terms? ............ 145
BIBLIOGRAPHY ............ 145
EXERCISES ............ 146

## CHAPTER 14 (Catherine A. Bowman)
### STANDARDIZATION ... 147
- 14.0 What are Technical Standards? ... 147
- 14.1 Scope of Technical Standards ... 147
- 14.2 Consensus ... 148
- 14.3 Standards in the Field of Terminology ... 148
- 14.4 Linguistic Standardization ... 149
- 14.5 Who Standardizes Terminology? ... 150
- 14.6 Which Terms Need to be Standardized? ... 152
- 14.7 Dissemination of Standardized Terms ... 153
- 14.8 Terminology Standardization Process ... 153
- 14.9 Conclusion ... 158
- BIBLIOGRAPHY ... 158
- EXERCISES ... 159

## CHAPTER 15 (Catherine A. Bowman)
### DOCUMENTATION ... 161
- 15.0 Introduction ... 161
- 15.1 Documentation and Terminology ... 161
- 15.2 Documentation and Usage ... 161
- 15.3 Available Resources ... 164
- 15.4 Evaluating Documentation ... 166
- 15.5 Terminology Reference Library ... 166
- 15.6 Documentalist ... 169
- 15.7 Corpus ... 170
- 15.8 Evaluating References ... 172
- 15.9 Useful Addresses ... 173
- BIBLIOGRAPHY ... 177
- EXERCISES ... 178

## CHAPTER 16 (Andy Lauriston)
### TERMINOLOGY AND THE COMPUTER ... 179
- 16.0 Introduction ... 179
- 16.1 Term Banks ... 179
- 16.2 Terminology File Management Systems ... 181
- 16.3 Terminology Files and Machine-Aided Translation ... 184
- 16.4 Machine-Aided Terminological Research ... 184
- 16.5 TERMINO—A More Promising Approach ... 189
- 16.6 A Proviso or Two ... 190
- BIBLIOGRAPHY ... 191
- EXERCISES ... 192

### INDEX ... 193

# CHAPTER 1

# WHAT IS TERMINOLOGY?

## 1.0 Introduction

There is no real consensus on the concept of terminology. Theorists and practitioners view the subject in distinctly different ways. There are many reasons for this, as we will see. One reason stems from the fact that terminology has borrowed from other, older fields, particularly semantics, lexicology and lexicography. As a result, some consider it part of these established linguistic disciplines.

Be that as it may, phenomenal advances in science and technology and growing communication among different language communities have created a serious need for new means of expression. Terminology, as we know it today, has evolved and developed in response to that need.

## 1.1 Beginnings of Modern Terminology

### 1.1.1 Advances in Science and Technology

Our age has witnessed staggering developments in science and technology. The frontiers of knowledge have been pushed back in many fields—genetics, space exploration, information science, telecommunications. All of the inventions and discoveries have generated the need for a vast number of terms: all new concepts need to be named.

### 1.1.2 Growing Communication Among Language Communities

The need for new terms, although significant in any one language, greatly increases when two or more language communities are in contact. For a given concept in one language, the equivalent must be identified in the others. Since every language reflects a different view of reality, the system of equivalent concepts and expressions must be established with discernment to respect the integrity of the languages involved. This approach to living terminology is clearly at odds with one school of thought, which maintains that problems of equivalence can be overcome by creating technical and scientific terminology common to a number of different languages.

### 1.1.3 Divergent Views of Terminology

Such disagreement on the nature and purpose of terminology was bound to create confusion. Without a consensus on suitable work methods and quality standards, many of the early "terminological" works rolling off the press fell very short of meeting a real need for means of expression.

Some practitioners, concerned that the proliferation of new terms would impede effective communication, saw terminology as a means of standardizing. For them, its purpose is essentially to prescribe the use of some terms and discourage that of others.

For many scholars of linguistics and lexicology, terminology is tantamount to technical lexicography. For them, its purpose is to research the basic terms specific to a field, rigorously define them, and classify them for retrieval.

Some schools of terminology believe their role is to prepare exhaustive word lists, without defining the terms or classifying the concepts. This approach in no way meets a need for special or technical communication. Moreover, in a translation context, these lists can prove extremely misleading because they offer no means of evaluating equivalence.

## 1.1.4 Meanings of *Terminology*

*Terminology* originally referred to the technical terms[1] and expressions used in an art, a science or a specialized subject. This meaning is still very much alive in English today.

*Terminology* later took on a broader meaning to refer to the investigation of such special or technical terms. In this sense, terminology involves the systematic research and identification of the terms specific to a subject field[2] and the concepts they represent.

Perhaps what best differentiates terminology from a related discipline like lexicography is its approach. The terminologist is concerned with finding the term that represents a given concept, the lexicographer, the meaning of a word. The question the terminologist is most likely to ask is "What's the **name** of the thing that . . . ?", whereas the lexicographer, "What does word X **mean**?". Thus, terminology encodes concepts, i.e. identifies their name, whereas lexicography decodes words, i.e. explains their meaning.

Since terminology is aimed at locating terms to facilitate communication, research efforts must be focused on the needs of the user. It is the user's needs that determine, to a large extent, the subject area to be investigated and the choice of work methods.

---

1. The distinction generally drawn between terms and words may be summed up as follows: "The items which are characterised by special reference within a discipline are the *terms* of that discipline and collectively they form its *terminology*; those which function in general reference over a variety of codes we call simply *words* and their totality the *vocabulary*." (J.C. Sager, D. Dungworth and P.F. McDonald, *English Special Languages: Principles and Practice in Science and Technology*, p. 75.)

2. A topic or field of knowledge which forms the subject of a terminological investigation.

## 1.2 Definition of Terminology

Alain Rey recommended that a distinction be drawn between the theoretical and practical aspects of terminology, i.e. that *terminology* refer to classes of objects and their designation, and *terminography* to the gathering, storage and dissemination of information on terms.[3] Although interesting, this distinction has not firmly taken root and therefore cannot form the basis of a definition of terminology.

We can nonetheless attempt a general definition that, while emphasizing the practical aspect of terminology, does not negate the theoretical. Accordingly, terminology can be defined as a discipline aimed at systematically identifying specialized terms in the context in which they are used, analyzing the concepts they represent in that context, and creating and standardizing terms if need be, to meet the user's need for means of expression.

### 1.2.1 Terminology—A Discipline

Terminology is a linguistic discipline which has developed theoretical guidelines to govern its practice and well-defined work methods to ensure the validity of its products.

### 1.2.2 Work Methods

There are four basic methods used in terminological work: term identification, contextual analysis, term creation and standardization. These methods are outlined briefly below and discussed at length in subsequent chapters.

---

3. This recommendation is found in "Terminologies and terminographies," in *La banque des mots* 10 (1975). Although Alain Rey's remarks were directed at the French *terminologie* and *terminographie*, they could just as easily apply to the English *terminology* and *terminography*.

### 1.2.2.1 Term Identification

When reading a specialized text or studying a real-life situation, the terminologist must be able to identify the terms specific to the subject field. This requires an excellent command of the general language and a knowledge of the field. A firm grasp of the general language enables the terminologist to sift out all non-specialized vocabulary, whereas a grounding in the subject and an overview of its conceptual framework allow him or her to pinpoint the specialized terms and record them by subfield.

The terminologist researches all means of expression peculiar to a field: simple terms, complex terms and phrases. Say, for example, a team of terminologists were conducting research in the field of office automation and wanted to identify all the terms specific to the field in the selected documentation. On what criteria would they base their choice of terms? How would they differentiate words from terms? After all, general-language words are often pressed into service as terms: the word *garbage* in general language and the term *garbage* in computer science have the same form but distinctly different meanings. In the case of complex terms and phrases, how would they decide where a particular term begins and ends?

### Simple Terms

Simple terms are one-word units which can be different parts of speech. Each represents a single concept in a subject field. *Architecture* (n.), *interconnection* (n.), *to query* (v.), *to execute* (v.), *dedicated* (adj.) and *interactive* (adj.) are examples of simple terms in office automation.

### Complex Terms

Complex terms are made up of two or more words. Like simple terms, they represent a single concept in a given field and can be different parts of speech. *Desktop publishing* (n.), *computer-aided design* (n.), *integrated services digital network* (n.), *double-sided double-density diskette* (n.), *to fine tune* (v.) and *user-friendly* (adj.) are examples of complex terms in office automation. Elimination of any one word in a complex unit would change the concept: *desktop publishing* and *publishing* have quite different meanings, as do *user-friendly* and *friendly*.

**Terminological Phrases**

Although phrasal units are never used as main entries by the lexicographer, they hold particular interest for the terminologist, as they constitute turns of phrase characteristically used in a special field. Examples of phrases in office automation include *to automate office procedures* (verbal), *connected to a central switch* (participial), *in binary notation* (prepositional), *in broadcast mode* (prepositional).

### 1.2.2.2 Contextual Analysis

Term identification is only one step in the research process and would be of little use on its own. The terminologist has to go on to determine the meaning of each term by analyzing the context in which it is found. Contextual analysis involves delimiting the context in which a term appears and pinpointing the semantic features, i.e. elements of meaning, it contains. A context is considered defining, explanatory or merely associative, depending on the quality and quantity of the semantic features it provides.

### 1.2.2.3 Term Creation

In bilingual terminology, new concepts may be named in one language and not in the other, or a reality specific to one language community may be foreign to the other. In such cases, the terminologist can create terms to fill the gaps, but must be well versed in term formation techniques (see Chapter 13, *TERM FORMATION*) and have a good knowledge of the special language to which the newly created term will belong.

The terminologist's role is, first and foremost, to identify existing terms, not to invent new ones. Coining a new term is warranted only when all available sources have been researched and the evidence indicates that there is no term in the target language for the concept under study.

### 1.2.2.4 Standardization

For some professionals, terminological research and standardization go hand in hand. Terminologists can, no doubt, make a valuable contribution to the standardization process, in view of the nature of their work and rigour of their methods. Their contribution can help make decisions about standardizing certain terms less arbitrary; this is particularly important when usage is being prescribed. Terminologists can nonetheless practise descriptive terminology without ever becoming involved in standardization.

### 1.2.3 Specialized Terms

Almost all fields of human endeavour have their own special language: the arts, science, business, economics, law, medicine.[4] The lexicon of a special language contains both general-language words and terms with special reference. Terminology is concerned with researching specialized terms, not general-language vocabulary.

### 1.2.4 Definitions and Contexts

Since the purpose of terminological work is to satisfy a real need for means of expression, terminologists must be aware of current usage. Their work would serve no purpose were

---

4. "Special languages ... are usually thought of as the means of expression of highly qualified subject specialists like engineers, physicians, lawyers, etc.... The fact that humbler occupations like nursing, book-keeping, and cooking and even hobbies also involve special areas of human interest and therefore also require and indeed have their own special languages is much less often acknowledged." (Sager, Dungworth and McDonald, p. 3.)

they to give the user depreciated or rare terminology. How do they determine usage? By researching terms in context.

In a *situational context*, the meaning of a term becomes clear when the terminologist connects the term with the concrete "thing" to which it refers.[5] In a written context, the meaning is not nearly as clear. The terminologist has to analyze the context and identify the semantic features it contains to gain an adequate understanding of the concept, but does not need to prepare a formal definition of it. A definition unquestionably elucidates a term's meaning, but stabilizes it and restricts it. The problem, of course, is that living language is continually changing; terms are constantly being given broader or narrower meanings.

Take *technology* for example. Webster's Third New International Dictionary (1986) defines it as:

> **2a** the science of the application of knowledge to practical purposes : applied science <the great American achievement has been ... less in science itself than in ~ and engineering — Max Lerner> **b** (1) : the application of scientific knowledge to practical purposes in a particular field <studies are also made of polymeric materials to dental ~ — *Report: Nat'l Bureau of Standards*> (2) : a technical method of achieving a practical purpose <a ~ for extracting petroleum from shale>

McGraw-Hill Dictionary of Scientific and Technical Terms (1978) defines *technology* as:

> Systematic knowledge of and its application to industrial processes . . . .

Now let's look at the following two contexts:

---

5. Say, for example, a terminologist were conducting research on dental techniques and having difficulty distinguishing *impression, mould* and *cast*, despite copious documentation. These concepts would became quite clear in a **situational context** were a dentist to show the terminologist the **impression** material which is placed over a patient's teeth, a **mould** which is made with that material and into which plaster is poured to make the **cast** or model.

> The word *technology* has multiple meanings. One is a systematized form of change—more formally, *technological innovation*. Thus, one of the aspects in which contemporary society differs from all its precursors is that there are a large group of technologists ... whose assigned task is to invent, develop and disseminate new ways of doing things and new kinds of things. (To make matters more complicated, *technology* ... can mean either the way of doing things or the things themselves.)[6]

> Once the technology that is being transferred has been developed, produced, and distributed, utilization can begin. Continued successful utilization of the newly transferred technology depends on whether it is properly operated, maintained, repaired, and kept up to date [7]

The first context overlaps with the dictionary definitions, but also extends beyond it, suggesting an important broadening of *technology* from a means of doing something to the end product itself. The second context confirms the new meaning: newly-developed equipment—the product of technology—is also referred to as *technology*.

These contexts provide the terminologist with enough information to decipher the term's current meaning in the source language and research the appropriate equivalent in the target language. Preparing a formal definition at this stage would needlessly slow down the research process.

Thus, terminologists must always be aware of usage and be on the lookout for new terms and new meanings. Lexicographic works are undeniably useful, but have limitations: they provide evidence of usage that is not necessarily up to date, and they provide information that is out of context and thus has to be interpreted. Terminology is a dynamic discipline aimed at researching living language in the contexts in which it is used.

6. Michael Goldhaber, *Reinventing Technology: Policies for Democratic Values* (New York: Routledge & Kegan Paul Inc., 1986), p. 8.

7. Robert W. House, "Considerations for Transferring Technologies," *Technology, International Stability and Growth*, ed. S. Basheer Ahmed (New York: Associated Faculty Press, Inc., 1984), p. 108.

In bilingual and multilingual terminology, this approach is of the utmost importance. Terminologists must locate sufficient information on the meaning of the source-language term in context to research its target-language equivalent in context. Equivalence of semantic features in source- and target-language contexts, referred to as *textual correspondence* in comparative terminology, is required to establish equivalence of terms.

### 1.2.5 User's Need for Means of Expression

Terminologists orient their work according to the user's communication needs. These needs, which are many and varied, depend on the languages involved, the activities in question and the people engaged in them. The terminological needs of an advertiser are undoubtedly very different from those of a scientist. Nonetheless, all users of terminology—no matter who they are or what language they speak—are constantly faced with the same problem: knowing what something is called or what to call something.

The user's need for terminology necessarily raises the question of access to information. In what form should terminological information be made available to those who need it?

### 1.2.6 Terminology Records

At the end of a research assignment, terminologists used to enter their findings on manual terminology records. These records could accommodate all reference information (sources and dates), illustrate equivalence of entries and concepts through corresponding contexts, and indicate the fields and subfields in which the terms were used.

### 1.2.7 Terminological Media

Manual terminology records were more working documents than means of disseminating terminological information, and were included in manual terminology files. Today, records are generally entered into computerized terminology databases, or used as a basis for preparing vocabularies or glossaries.

### 1.2.7.1 Terminology Files and Databases

In manual terminology files—bilingual or multilingual—records were accessed by looking up the source- or target-language entry. However, for the terminologist to access records using key terms other than the entry, the main record had to be reproduced or a cross-reference had to be created for every key term used. Obviously such a system was totally impractical for a file containing thousands of records.

One of the many advantages of computerized terminology databases is that they do offer multiple access to information, without the information itself having to be reproduced. They can also store vast amounts of data, and allow for extremely fast information retrieval. As a result, they have virtually replaced the old manual systems.

### 1.2.7.2 Vocabularies

When subject-field research is carried out for a wide audience or for users unfamiliar with terminological methods, the findings are usually published in vocabulary form, with the items listed in alphabetical order.

The body of a vocabulary generally contains the source-language entry and the target-language equivalents in the case of bilingual or multilingual research, a concise definition formulated from the contextual information found in the source and target languages, and an indication of the subfield based on the subject-field breakdown. The front matter often provides information on the subject field and research methodology. The back matter typically includes alphabetical indices for any source-language synonyms and all target-language equivalents, as well as a bibliography of the main sources consulted. Vocabularies are published in hard copy or made available in computerized form.

### 1.2.7.3 Glossaries

In some cases, terminological information is published in the form of glossaries, which provide an alphabetical listing of terms specific to a discipline and their target-language equivalents. This medium is intended primarily for audiences who have a reasonably good knowledge of the subject field and therefore do not need definitions. Although the information in a glossary is scant, it can be supplemented with usage labels and an indication of the subfields.

Vocabulary and glossary formats are sometimes combined. In such cases, the key concepts are defined and the rest of the terminological information is presented in glossary form.

### 1.2.7.4 Didactic Media

Subject-field outlines and explanatory illustrations are also used to teach the terminology of a field to uninitiated audiences. Outlines provide a concise description of the subject field and give terminological information as the concepts are presented. Illustrations offer a particularly useful means of portraying an object and identifying its component parts. A good illustration enables the reader to make a clear connection between a term and concept, and serves as a useful complement to other terminological data.

## 1.3 Conclusion

The concept of terminology introduced in this chapter may be summarized as follows:

**CONCEPT OF TERMINOLOGY**

| Nature | Methods | Subject | Purpose | Media |
|---|---|---|---|---|
| Linguistic discipline | Identifying, analyzing, creating and standardizing | Specialized terms | To meet the user's need for means of expression | Terminology records, vocabularies, glossaries and terminology databases |

# BIBLIOGRAPHY

CSA Standard CAN/CSA-Z781-92. *Terminology—Vocabulary.* Toronto: Canadian Standards Association, June 1992.

Felbert, Helmut. *Terminology Manual.* Paris: Unesco, 1984.

Goffin, Roger. "Pour une formation universitaire *sui generis* du traducteur." *Meta* 16 (March to June 1971): 57–68.

Hoffmann, L. "Terminology and LSP." In *Terminologies for the Eighties.* General ed. International Information Centre for Terminology (Infoterm), Issue ed. Wolfgang Nedobity. Federal Republic of Germany: K.G. Saur Verlag KG, 1982, pp. 391–401.

Palmer, F.R. *Semantics.* 2nd ed. Cambridge, England: Cambridge University Press, 1981.

Picht, Heribert, and Jennifer Draskau. *Terminology: An Introduction.* Surrey, England: The University of Surrey, 1985.

Rondeau, Guy. *Introduction à la terminologie.* Chicoutimi, Québec: Gaëtan Morin éditeur, 1984.

Sager, Juan C. *A Practical Course in Terminology Processing.* Philadelphia: John Benjamins Publishing Company, 1990.

Sager, Juan C., David Dungworth, and Peter F. McDonald. *English Special Languages: Principles and Practice in Science and Technology.* Germany: Oscar Brandstetter Verlag KG, 1980.

*Vocabulary of Terminology.* Ottawa: Terminology Directorate, Secretary of State, 1983.

Zgusta, Ladislav. *Manual of Lexicography.* Prague: Academia, Publishing House of the Czechoslovak Academy of Sciences, 1971.

# EXERCISES

1. Compare the definition of terminology provided in section 1.2 with the following:

   "Terminology science: Inter- and transdisciplinary field of knowledge dealing with concepts and their representations (terms, symbols, etc.)."

2. Identify the simple terms, complex terms and terminological phrases in a short text on a subject of interest to you.

3. Research and compare the concepts of general language and special languages. What place does terminology hold in special languages?

4. What is the difference between vocabulary and terminology?

# CHAPTER 2

# THE SITUATION IN TERMINOLOGY

## 2.0 Introduction

Louis Guilbert emphasized the social function of terminology, thereby acknowledging its fundamental role: to meet the user's need for appropriate means of expression. He saw "terminological discourse" in a pragmatic light, as used by people to refer to extralinguistic reality.[1] In written and oral communication, an individual's choice of terms is influenced by his or her situational context. As a result, the same concept may be labelled differently in different situations. Researchers may refer to the preliminary survey they conduct to determine the precise scope and objectives of their research as a *dry run* in conversation, but as an *exploratory study* in their written report; advertisers may call the total number of television viewers and radio listeners exposed to a message during a predetermined period *total impacts*, while broadcast researchers may refer to them as the *gross audience*; the device for transmitting and receiving radio waves may be called an *aerial* in England, but an *antenna* in the United States. In each of these cases, the concept is the same, but the label changes according to the socioprofessional or geographic context.

Sager (and many other scholars, for that matter) agrees that the situational context has an important bearing on the choice of appropriate expression. He points out that "the user-oriented or pragmatic approach requires investigation both of the circumstances under which individuals use language, and the potential or functions of the language they use. In both there are socially determined elements . . . . In his choice of means of expression the individual is influenced by the

---

1. Louis Guilbert, "Terminologie et linguistique," p. 212.

subject he is talking about, his place in society and his geographical location."[2]

Thus, in any terminological research, the situational context must be determined before term and concept can be properly investigated. As Palmer puts it, "living languages must not be treated like dead ones, torn from their context of situation, but seen as used by people . . . . "[3]

## 2.1 Situation and Living Language

This view of the situational context in terminological research is at odds with any assumption that the terminology of a field can be established *a priori* and consist of universals applicable to all types of discourse. Such a terminology, although perhaps intended to meet an ideal of effective communication, is unnatural and incompatible with living language, no matter how technical or specialized it may be.

## 2.2 Situation and View of Reality

Expanding on Sapir's theory that the world in which we live "is to a large extent unconsciously built upon the language habits of the group,"[4] Whorf argued that language is "the shaper of ideas" and that we view the world along lines laid down by our native languages.[5] Differences in each language's "view of reality" can create significant difficulties in determining equivalence, which the situational context can ultimately help overcome. For example, the telephone service which enables subscribers to make calls to an off-hook telephone to listen for noises in a room is referred to as *babyphone service* in English and *service de télésurveillance acoustique* in French. The English term zeros in on the subject

---

2. J.C. Sager, D. Dungworth, and P.F. McDonald, *English Special Languages: Principles and Practice in Science and Technology*, pp. 6–7.

3. F.R. Palmer, *Semantics*, p. 51.

4. *Ibid.*, p. 45.

5. *Ibid.*

being listened to (a baby), whereas the French emphasizes the reason for listening (surveillance). Identifying these terms in context offers a means of ensuring that they represent the same concept and are therefore equivalent.

## 2.3 Comparative Terminology

The terms identified in bilingual or multilingual research are not literal translations. French does not have literal translations for colourful English advertising terms like *man-bite-dog technique* and *bombshell wipe*. English does not have literal translations for figurative French broadcasting terms like *fourgon* and *locomotive*. Living terminology can be very idiomatic—a fact that must be duly considered in all terminological work.

## 2.4 Situation and Usage

Despite its merits, living terminology can pose a number of problems. Some rapidly evolving fields are fraught with synonyms, polysemous expressions and obscure formulations which can impede effective communication. Taking the situational context into account in no way prevents the terminologist from seeking solutions to such problems and making carefully weighed decisions concerning usage.

## 2.5 Situation and Users

Given the importance of the situational context in terminological research, users can and should play an important role in the investigation of terminologies. They can provide invaluable insight into the need for research, the situational context, the conceptual framework of their field, and so on. It is essential to bear in mind that terminologies are not the exclusive domain of terminologists. Terminologists are not there to protect the terminologies with which they work, but to provide users with suitable communication tools.

## 2.6 Situation and Work Method

This pragmatic approach to terminology requires that all terminological work be based on a real need. This need must be determined in collaboration with the user, and the situational context must be clearly defined. The framework of the research—target audience, level of language, scope, specific field and subfields—will depend on the needs voiced and the situation in question.

### 2.6.1 Target Audience and Level of Language

The framework of the research should be determined at the outset, otherwise a good deal of time and energy can be wasted. Attempting to be exhaustive when the situation does not actually call for it can greatly reduce a terminologist's productivity. Identifying the target audience and level of language is essential to ensure that the terminology researched adequately meets the user's needs. A physician, for example, would not be interested in using the same terms as a writer of medical articles for a lay audience.

### 2.6.2 Data Gathering

Once the framework of the research has been determined, sources of information—oral and written—must be located. Appropriate oral informants can guide the terminologist through the maze of concepts for which names must be found, and establish the essential link between the various concepts and the extralinguistic reality they represent. Written sources, including handbooks and standards, provide evidence of usage and constitute a stable medium for "situational" terminology. Lexicographic documents—dictionaries and encyclopedias—can also prove useful, but should be consulted primarily on an *ad hoc* basis to clarify certain concepts or evaluate certain terms.

## 2.6.3 Signs and Labelling

Specialized language is often compressed into succinct terms or phrases when used on signs, packaging and labels. Determining the equivalent of these expressions in another language can pose some unusual problems. How, for example, do you establish the French equivalent of *on/off* appearing on a machine lever, *Do not X-ray* printed on photographic packaging and *No admission* posted at the entrance to a site? Only a comparative study of the situations in which these terms are used can provide a satisfactory answer. A literal translation, so often used in bilingual countries, does not offer a functional solution. One of the first warnings printed on cigarette packages in English Canada read *Danger to health increases with amount smoked*. This phrase was translated literally into French and the result was unwieldy. The phrase appearing on cigarette packages in France at the time was simply *Abus dangereux*. Same meaning, but a completely different formulation.

## 2.6.4 Selection of Terms

The situational context helps guide the selection of terms to be extracted from a corpus and included in a terminological work. A terminologist preparing a vocabulary of pulp and paper terms, for example, may wonder whether a particular chemical term should be selected for inclusion. Only the situation can indicate whether the term is commonly or rarely used in the field. By using the situation as a guide, the terminologist can avoid the pitfall of including inappropriate terms in the work and excluding relevant ones.

## 2.7 Situation and Standardization

Situational terminology is aimed at describing usage, whereas standardization, at prescribing usage. Approaches to researching situational terminology and to establishing standardized terminology may seem contradictory. However, this is not the case; these approaches can and must be complementary.

### 2.7.1 Overcoming the Limitations of Situational Terminology

Situational terminology is unplanned and can therefore be "unruly". Terms specific to a subject field can be polysemous within that field. *Picking*, for example, has three different meanings in textiles: harvesting cotton, snagging and weaving. Evolving fields are often replete with synonyms. *Psychotropic drugs*, for example, which were the subject of much learned discussion when psychopharmacology emerged in the early 1950s, were also called: *psychopharmaca, psychodrugs, psychopharmacologic agents, psychotherapeutic drugs, psychopharmaceuticals, phrenopraxics, phrenotropic drugs, psychotropic agents* and *psychoactive substances*.[6] Some subject fields borrow words or terms and give them a meaning which bears little or no relation to their original meaning. For example, in his article on the production of scientific terms, Arthur Caso explains that

> *quark* has been added to the lexicon of physics as the name of a newly hypothesized atomic particle. *Quark* was coined by Murray Gell-Mann, who explained its derivation during an appearance on Nigel Calder's 1977 BBC television production *The Key to the Universe*: 'The mathematics clearly called for a set of underlying elementary objects—at that time we needed three types of them—elementary objects that could be combined three at a time in different ways to make all the heavy particles we knew.... I needed a name for them and called them *quarks*, after the taunting cry of the gulls, *Three quarks for Muster Mark*, from *Finnegan's Wake*, by the Irish writer James Joyce.'[7]

The author goes on to mention a number of other equally whimsical borrowings including *truth* and *beauty* for the fifth and sixth quarks.

---

6. *Principles of Psychopharmacology*, 2nd ed., edited by William G. Clark and Joseph del Giudice (New York: Academic Press, 1978), pp. 1 and 39.

7. Arthur Lewis Caso, "The Production of New Scientific Terms," *American Speech* 55 (1980): 101.

Standardization can help overcome some of the limitations of situational terminology by narrowing the meaning of polysemous expressions, reducing the number of synonyms in certain cases, and ensuring that internal borrowings preserve some degree of their original motivation.

### 2.7.2 Making Standardization Less Arbitrary

Despite its shortcomings, much can be said in favour of situational terminology. Situational terminology is living terminology. It takes into account the social, professional and geographic variations in a special language, thereby respecting that language's richness and resources. Even more compelling is the fact that it successfully meets a wide range of communication needs by providing users with situationally-appropriate forms of expression.

Standardized terminologies cannot hope to promote effective communication if they disregard living language. If standardization ultimately gives rise to artificial terminology cut off from living language, it seriously misses the mark. Further on, in the chapter on standardization, we will see how the imperatives of situational terminology can be reconciled with those of standardization.

# BIBLIOGRAPHY

Cruse, D.A. *Lexical Semantics*, especially Chapter 1, "A Contextual Approach to Lexical Semantics." Cambridge, England: Cambridge University Press, 1986.

Dubois, Claude. "La spécificité de la définition en terminologie." In *Actes du sixième colloque international de terminologie*. Pointe-au-Pic, Québec: Gouvernement du Québec, 1979, pp. 45–59.

Guilbert, Louis. "Terminologie et linguistique." In *Textes choisis de terminologie*. Ed. G. Rondeau and H. Felber. Québec: Groupe interdisciplinaire de recherche scientifique et appliquée en terminologie (GIRSTERM), 1981, pp. 201–219.

Palmer, F.R. *Semantics*. 2nd ed. especially Chapter 3, "Context and Reference." Cambridge, England: Cambridge University Press, 1981.

Rey, Alain. "Les fonctions de la terminologie : du social au théorique." In *Actes du sixième colloque OLF-STQ de terminologie*. Montréal: Gouvernement du Québec, 1985, pp. 87–108.

Sager, Juan C., David Dungworth, and Peter F. McDonald. *English Special Languages: Principles and Practice in Science and Technology*. Germany: Oscar Brandstetter Verlag KG, 1980.

# EXERCISES

1. How does the situation-oriented approach to research affect the work methods used in terminology?

2. Does the situation-oriented approach prevent users from becoming involved in the investigation of terminology? Discuss.

3. Are dictionaries and encyclopedias useful in researching situational terminology? Discuss.

# CHAPTER 3

# TERMINOLOGY, SEMANTICS AND LEXICOGRAPHY

### SHIRLEY LEDREW

## 3.0 Introduction

Terminology, as we know it today, is a relatively new discipline. As a result, it tends to be confused with other linguistic disciplines concerned with the lexical aspects of language. Terminology has been variously described as technical lexicography or as semantics applied to technical language. Although closely related to these disciplines, terminology differs significantly from them. Terminology is an independent discipline which has developed to meet the accelerating need for specialized means of expression. In this chapter, terminology will be compared with semantics and lexicography in order to differentiate it and clarify its specificity.

## 3.1 Terminology and Semantics

### 3.1.1 General Concept of Semantics

In its broadest accepted sense, semantics[1] is the study of the relationship between the linguistic sign and the object to which it refers. The semanticist is interested primarily in discovering how a particular sign (word) came to be associated with a specific referent (thing), to learn, for example, why a chair is called a *chair*.

Two main approaches have developed in semantics: the *historical* or *diachronic*, and the *descriptive* or *synchronic*. The

---

1. *Semantics*, in this context, is short for *lexical semantics* (as opposed to *syntactic*).

traditional approach to investigating the connection between word and thing is historical. To explain, for example, why a cold-blooded aquatic vertebrate with gills is called a *fish*, the semanticist examines the etymology of the word to find that it is derived from the Old English *fisc* and Old Frisian *fisk* and is cognate with the Latin word *piscis*.

Once the etymology has been established, the semanticist analyzes the link between the initial meaning of *fish* and the other meanings the word has acquired over time. From its first meaning of living animal, the semanticist shows that *fish* took on an inanimate meaning to refer to the flesh of the animal eaten for food, through a shift in application, a figurative abstract meaning to represent a cold person, through metonymy (shared typical characteristic of being cold), and acquired a number of figurative concrete meanings to designate: a constellation, through analogy of form; a piece of hard wood used to strengthen the mast of a ship, also through analogy of form; a casing-like part of a variable-depth sonar system, again through analogy of form; a process for recovering lost mining equipment from a borehole, through analogy with the action of catching fish; and an oceanographic sensing device towed by a ship, also through analogy with the action of catching fish.

The contemporary approach, based on the work of Swiss linguist Ferdinand de Saussure, is descriptive. In this method, meanings are viewed as systems. One meaning can have several signs (synonymy); and one sign can have several meanings, the dates of which are irrelevant because the old and new meanings survive side by side in the form of polysemy.[2]

In diachronic and synchronic semantics, *fish* is a polysemous word whose various meanings can be charted as follows:

---

2. S. Ullmann, *The Principles of Semantics*, p. 37.

## MEANINGS OF *FISH*

| LITERAL ||
|---|---|
| **Animate** | **Inanimate** |
| cold-blooded aquatic vertebrate with gills | flesh of the animal eaten for food (shift in application) |
| **FIGURATIVE** ||
| **Abstract** | **Concrete** |
| cold person (metonymy) | constellation (analogy of form) |
| | piece of hard wood used to strengthen the mast of a ship (analogy of form) |
| | casing-like part of a variable-depth sonar system (analogy of form) |
| | process for recovering lost mining equipment from a borehole (analogy with action of catching fish) |
| | oceanographic sensing device towed by a ship (analogy with action of catching fish) |

All these meanings, literal and figurative, animate and inanimate, concrete and abstract, together constitute the semantic range of the word *fish* in modern English.

### 3.1.2 Linguistic Sign and Referent in Terminology

The terminologist takes a different approach to the linguistic sign. The sign is viewed as a means of communication; as a result, all terminological inquiry begins by investigating the context in which a given sign is used, rather than by studying its etymology. In this respect, terminology is essentially synchronic. The relationship between a particular sign and its referent is of interest only insofar as the terminologist can categorically link the sign to the semantic features of the object to be named in a particular subject field.

A terminologist conducting research in the field of biology, for example, would determine that a cold-blooded aquatic vertebrate with gills is, in fact, called a *fish*. The fact that the term may have other meanings in other fields, while interesting, is not of primary concern. Similarly, a terminologist researching the terms used in geophysical exploration would note that an oceanographic sensing device towed behind a ship is called a *fish*.

For the semanticist, the word *fish* is associated with a basic meaning, cold-blooded aquatic vertebrate with gills, to which other meanings have subsequently been added according to the various relationships shown in the chart in 3.1.1.

A terminologist wishing to study all the meanings of the term *fish* would do so by subject field:

> **Biology**: the animal
>
> **Cuisine**: flesh of the animal eaten for food
>
> **Interpersonal Communications**: cold person
>
> **Geophysical Exploration**: oceanographic sensing device towed behind a ship
>
> **Mining**: process of recovering lost drilling tools from a borehole
>
> **Shipbuilding**: (1) piece of hard wood used to strengthen the mast of a ship; (2) casing-like part of a variable-depth sonar system.

However, the terminologist would not be concerned about the relationship between the different meanings in the different subject fields.

### 3.1.3 Relationship between Terminology and Semantics

As the foregoing examples illustrate, the semanticist studies all the different meanings that have evolved over time or that coexist for a given word, while the terminologist seeks to associate a number of semantic features with a given label in a given subject field.

The terminologist borrows methods of analysis from the semanticist to identify the full range of semantic features or characteristics of a concept, but does not attempt to explain the use of a particular term to represent a particular meaning. The terminologist aims to establish a link between concept and label in a given context or communication situation, while taking into account two important aspects of this link: synonymy and polysemy. In shipbuilding, for example, the casing-like part of a variable-depth sonar system known as a *fish* is also called a *sonar body*. Moreover, *fish* has two different meanings in this subject field. Recording synonyms and cases of polysemy within a specific field is an essential part of terminological work.

The semanticist investigates language by semantic field in order to identify and organize related ideas. In so doing, the semanticist groups together words that share common characteristics. For example, under the general word *seat*, the semanticist would include such specific words as *chair, armchair, love seat, sofa, bench* and *stool*, which all share the following characteristics or semantic field: a piece of furniture designed for sitting.

For the terminologist, the purpose of studying terms that belong to the same semantic field is to draw distinctions between concepts that, being related, are often confused. The terminologist therefore seeks to identify all the characteristics that differentiate each term in a given semantic field. This process is particularly useful in studying pseudo-synonyms (discussed in Chapter 12, *SYNONYMY*).

### 3.1.4 Semantics and Term Formation

Semantic change is one of the two main ways in which new terms are formed. As we have seen in the case of *fish* in section 3.1.1, semantic change alters the meaning of an established word through a number of different processes, including analogy and metonymy.[3] The terminologist can contribute to the term formation process by helping ensure that new coinages follow time-honored patterns of semantic change.

### 3.1.5 Summary

Semantics and terminology differ in nature and purpose. Semantics is intralinguistic, because it deals with language as a system. Terminology, however, is extralinguistic, because it deals primarily with communication in context. The terminologist works with special languages, viewing them as means of communication, not as systems.

Both disciplines study the relationship between the linguistic sign and its referents, but from different angles. In semantics, the word-thing relationship is explained by analyzing the occurrences of polysemy and by grouping together related words that belong to the same semantic field. In terminology, the sign-referent relationship is investigated from an *onomasiological*[4] point of view: the terminologist researches and records the name of a concept, without attempting to explain the connection. If a particular sign represents more than one concept in a subject field, the terminologist pinpoints the characteristics of each concept to differentiate them. If a given concept has more than one sign in a special field, the terminologist records the synonyms and distinguishes them according to the guidelines provided in Chapter 12, *SYNONYMY*. When a term is created for a new

---

3. See Chapter 13, *TERM FORMATION*, for a full discussion of the various processes of semantic change.

4. Of or relating to a method of investigation that starts with the concept and attempts to discover the corresponding sign or signs.

concept, the terminologist can contribute to the process by offering advice on established term formation techniques.

To sum up, semantics and terminology differ in the way they view the relationship between the sign and its referents. Semantics *explains* this relationship, terminology *applies* it.

## 3.2 Terminology and Lexicography

Before we look at the similarities and differences between terminology and lexicography, a definition of lexicography is in order. Lexicography generally refers to the study and practice of dictionary-making.

### 3.2.1 Nature of the Two Disciplines

By their very nature, terminology and lexicography are closely related: the raw material of both disciplines is words. However, the lexicographer investigates the entire lexicon,[5] i.e. the total stock available to a community for its communication needs, whereas the terminologist researches specialized vocabulary, i.e. the limited stock specific to a field of knowledge and used in a particular communication context.

The link between terminology and the communication context is based on the need to provide users with appropriate means of expression. To meet this need, the terminologist identifies the characteristics of a concept represented by a term in a specific situation; it is the situation which gives a term its special shade of meaning. This approach enables the terminologist to remain attuned to the changes inherent in living language and to bridge the gap between dictionaries and usage. The terminologist investigates the meaning of terms *in vivo*, whereas the lexicographer pins down all the meanings of a word to study it *in vitro*.

---

5. All words in a language, including nouns, verbs, adjectives and adverbs as well as function words—articles, prepositions and conjunctions.

The extralinguistic context of things to be named is used by the terminologist to structure the vocabulary of a subject field, which is viewed as a set of signs firmly rooted in reality.[6] A terminology developed without constant concern for the situational context, experience, and reality would in no way meet the need for which it is intended.

### 3.2.2 Objective

Terminology and lexicography differ, first and foremost, in objective. The terminologist begins with a concept and proceeds to research its sign, whereas the lexicographer works in the opposite direction, starting with a sign and proceeding to investigate the concept or concepts it represents. As already noted, terminology is aimed at meeting the user's need for means of expression and communication. Users of terminology are in search of a name, not necessarily a definition; they are looking for the verbal means to encode their message. Users of dictionaries have a different objective; they need tools to help them learn the meaning of words they know but do not understand, so they can decode a message.

These different objectives explain the different methodologies used by practitioners of the two disciplines.

### 3.2.3 Work Methods

#### 3.2.3.1 Establishing a Nomenclature

The lexicographer researches all the words in a language and all meanings of each word in all communication situations. The terminologist, however, identifies the terms belonging to a given subject and falling within the study framework. To establish the nomenclature of textiles, the terms belonging to the field or a limited area of the industry must be identified, taking into account the communication situations specified by the research framework.

---

6. See Chapter 6, section 6.1.5, *Preparing a Breakdown of the Subject Field*.

In practice, this difference in approach will result in a nomenclature that contains not only terms representing the basic concepts of a subject field, but all means of expression peculiar to it: simple terms, complex terms and terminological phrases—phrases that are characteristic expressions used in a given special language (see 1.2.2.1, *Term Identification*). Phrasal forms will be included in the nomenclature, even if their degree of lexicalization is relatively low (see 7.1.2, *Degree of Lexicalization*).

### 3.2.3.2   Term Identification

Terminology units therefore differ from lexical units. Since terminology units are researched in the context of written or spoken messages, they may appear in a less lexicalized form than lexical units.

Terminology units must nonetheless be sufficiently lexicalized to be differentiated from units of discourse, i.e. accidental groupings of words. A grouping like *trailer which can be converted into a dwelling* would be regarded by the terminologist as a definition, not a terminology unit.

### 3.2.3.3   Methods of Analysis

Lexicographical analysis is aimed at discovering all the meanings of a word and establishing its complete semantic profile. To this end, the lexicographer carries out extensive research to identify meanings and arrange them in a logical order. The entire analysis process must enable the lexicographer to formulate a definition, which is semantically equivalent to the meanings of the lexical unit as identified in the various contexts selected, and supported by examples of usage.

Terminological analysis, for its part, is aimed at determining the characteristics of the concept represented by a term identified when the nomenclature for a field is being established. The context in which a term is located supplies the semantic features that enable the terminologist to link concept and term, to research the equivalent in another language, and provide the user with the correct label for a concept. The main purpose of terminological analysis is to identify semantic content; rather than seeking definitions, the terminologist attempts to identify such semantic features as nature, purpose, function and material.

### 3.2.4 Definition

This difference in approach also explains the difference between a terminological and a lexicographical definition. A lexicographer's definition must provide a complete semantic profile of a word in all its accepted uses. A terminologist's definition condenses the semantic features of a term as it is used in a given real-life situation. When terminologists use a lexicographical definition, they must always refer to the situational context.

### 3.2.5 Key Information Media

The dictionary entry is the key information medium produced by the lexicographer. Since the main purpose of a dictionary is to teach users the meaning or meanings of words they do not fully understand, the writing of dictionary entries is governed by well-defined rules of a pedagogical nature. The main information in a dictionary entry includes the headword, preferred spelling, use of capitalization, pronunciation, part of speech, and sometimes etymology and encyclopedic information. The definition is an essential part of the entry. Defined meanings must be organized according to historical or logical criteria and illustrated with examples. In a French dictionary, entries for nouns often include derived phrasal forms: under *fer*, for example, will be found *fer à friser, fer à repasser, fer à souder*. In an English dictionary, derived phrases are usually entered as headwords as well.

Thus a dictionary entry is synthetic (constructed around a headword), pedagogical (specifying meanings and usage in written and spoken language), and exhaustive (providing all accepted meanings).

For a terminologist, the basic information medium is the terminology record, a document indicating observed contextual use. It contains the term for the object to be named and cites a context with sufficient information to provide a relatively clear idea of the concept represented. A record documents only one concept. Complex terms and terminological phrases are shown in their normal word order. Grammatical and usage labels are included only when significant, for example, when the part of speech could be ambiguous or when there are differences in geographic usage between the entry term and its synonyms. The subject field and subfields are always entered to indicate the communication situation.

Thus, a terminology record is monosemous (covering only one concept), situational (valid only for the context cited), and an encoding instrument (linking concept with term).

### 3.2.6  End Products

The end product of lexicographic work is the dictionary, a collection of words, usually in alphabetical order, under which the various entries are provided. A dictionary is a tool that stabilizes or fixes usage; it provides a "snapshot" of the lexicon at a given moment in its evolution. Two consecutive editions of the same dictionary will show changes: obsolete meanings will disappear and new ones will be added; however, whenever a dictionary entry is consulted, the user senses only permanence and stability.

The end product of terminological work is the file of terminology records, which is organized according to various parameters (see Chapter 10, *TERMINOLOGY RECORDS*). Such files may be simple cards filed alphabetically, or complex computerized files stored on CD-ROM, magnetic tape or diskette. A terminology file evolves continuously, growing in step with terminology research. If the file is to reflect current usage, it must be updated periodically to delete records that are no longer valid and include new ones that have been produced.

Various specialized vocabularies and glossaries can be published from terminology files. While they may be similar in form to lexicographic works, they are clearly terminological in orientation.

### 3.2.7 Summary

The following chart sums up the differences between terminology and lexicography.

**COMPARISON OF TERMINOLOGY AND LEXICOGRAPHY**

| POINTS OF COMPARISON | TERMINOLOGY | LEXICOGRAPHY |
| --- | --- | --- |
| Nature | Lexical discipline | Lexical discipline |
| Material | Vocabulary | Lexicon |
| Objective | To encode | To decode |
| Nomenclature | Specific | Global |
| Units identified | Simple terms, complex terms and terminological phrases | Mainly single and highly-lexicalized words |
| Features analyzed | Semantic features revealed by the context | All semantic features |
| Definition | A single concept | All meanings |
| Key information medium | Terminology record | Dictionary entry |
| End product | Terminology file | Dictionary |

# BIBLIOGRAPHY

Cruse, D.A. *Lexical Semantics*. Cambridge, England: Cambridge University Press, 1986.

Kipfer, Barbara Ann. *Workbook on Lexicography*. Exeter, England: A. Wheaton and Company Limited, 1984.

Landau, Sidney. *Dictionaries: The Art and Craft of Lexicography*. New York: Charles Scribner's Sons, 1984.

Palmer, F.R. *Semantics*. 2nd ed. Cambridge, England: Cambridge University Press, 1981.

Ullmann, Stephen. *The Principles of Semantics*. New York: Barnes & Noble, 1967.

Ullmann, Stephen. *Semantics: An Introduction to the Science of Meaning*. Oxford: Basil Blackwell, 1970.

Zgusta, L., ed. *Theory and Method in Lexicography: Western and Non-Western Perspectives*. South Carolina: Hornbeam Press Incorporated, 1980.

# EXERCISES

1. Select a term of interest to you and study it from a semantic, lexicographic and terminological standpoint.

2. How do the methods of analysis used in semantics, lexicography and terminology differ? Discuss.

3. Research and explain the difference between the words *lexicon* and *vocabulary* as used in this chapter.

# CHAPTER 4

# TERM AND CONCEPT

## 4.0 Introduction

To achieve its purpose—to meet the user's need for appropriate means of expression—terminological inquiry must clarify the relationship between a term and the concept it represents, i.e. between the *signifier* and the *signified*.

## 4.1 Signifier and Signified

One of the oldest views, expressed in Plato's dialogue *Cratylus*, is that the signifier is a word in language and the signified, the object in the world which it stands for. A more sophisticated view, held by some philosophers and linguists from ancient times up to modern day, is that the signifier and signified are related through the mediation of concepts in the mind.[1]

The nature of the link between a word in language, the extralinguistic reality it denotes and the concept it evokes in the mind remains a subject of copious debate among semanticists. Ferdinand de Saussure, one of the pioneers of modern linguistics, theorized that the signifier (uttered and written word) and the signified (concept) are linked by a psychological associative bond, and that both the sounds we utter and the objects in the world we talk about are somehow mirrored by concepts.[2]

While the so-called *semiotic triangle*, i.e. language symbol, thought or concept, and referent or object in the real world, is relevant in terminology, the focus of terminological investigation is more pragmatic. Terminological work is concerned, first and foremost, with researching the concepts that

---

1. F.R. Palmer, *Semantics*, pp. 17–24.

2. *Ibid.*, p. 24.

constitute a subject field and the names or labels thereof. Although the terminologist never loses sight of extra-linguistic reality, the primary objects of research are specialized concepts and the terms that represent them.

## 4.2 What is a Term?

A *term* or *terminology unit* is a word or expression that designates a *concept* specific to a subject field and the corresponding *object* in the world.

### 4.2.1 Morphologically Speaking

A terminology unit can be a *simple term, complex term* or *terminological phrase*. A simple term is a one-word unit which consists of a stem,[3] with or without affixes. *To coproduce* (v.), *commentator* (n.) and *monochrome* (adj.) are simple terms, despite the fact that they contain more than one morpheme.[4] *To coproduce* contains the stem *produce* and the prefix *co-*; *commentator*, the stem *comment* and the suffix *-ator*; and *monochrome*, the Greek combining form *mono* and the Greek noun *chrome*. These terms—used in the field of television production—are considered to be simple because the affixes (*co-* and *-ator*) and combining form (*mono*) they contain cannot occur as separate terms.

Complex terms are made up of two or more words with a grammatical relationship. Like simple terms, they can be different parts of speech. *Captive audience* (adj. + n. = n.), *laughmeter* (n. + n. = n.), *director-producer* (n. + n. = n.), *close-up* (adv. + prep. = adj.), *ultrawide-angle lens* (adv. + adj. + n. + n. = n.) and *to lip sync* (n. + v. = v.) are examples of complex terms used in television production. Like simple terms, complex terms represent a single concept. Elimination of any one element of a complex term would change the concept.

---

3. Word element which can be used as a term in itself or as the base of a derivative. (CSA Standard CAN/CSA-Z781-92, *Terminology—Vocabulary*, 5.5.5, p. 7.)

4. The smallest grammatical unit of language. (*Ibid.*, 5.5.3.5, p. 7.)

Phrases are characteristic means of expression used in a special language. They are made up of a group of words and have a higher syntactic function than simple or complex terms. *Request for copyright clearance* (nominal phrase), *to preempt a program* (infinitive phrase), *filmed on location* (participial phrase) and *on the air* (prepositional phrase) are examples of phrases in television production. Like simple and complex terms, terminological phrases represent a single concept in a special subject.

### 4.3 Concept

A concept peculiar to a field or discipline can be described by the aggregate of its essential characteristics. For example, we can describe the concept *watch* by identifying such characteristics as "having a face and hands", "being used to tell time", and "having a movement driven in any of several ways". These are *necessary characteristics*, but not sufficient to distinguish a *watch* from all other related concepts, i.e. other timepieces, so we have to add the characteristic of "being designed to be worn on a wristband, pin or chain". The necessary and sufficient characteristics of a concept, which enable us to distinguish it from all other concepts, are referred to as *essential*.

The essential characteristics of a concept need not be given in any particular order. The essential characteristics of *watch* above, for example, could be listed in any order and they would still be sufficient to describe the concept. In this respect, concept description differs from definition, which requires that essential characteristics be organized hierarchically.

### 4.4 Specificity to Subject Field

The terminologist always investigates terms in the context of the field to which they belong. General-language words are constantly being borrowed by different disciplines to name new concepts and designate new realities. In the process, their meaning is broadened, narrowed or otherwise changed; they are assigned, as it were, a new semantic load. For example, *furniture* in the urban planning term *street furniture* does not have the same meaning as it does in the general language, nor does *highway* in the computer communications term *information highway*. The concept represented by a term is specific to a subject field and must therefore be researched in the context of that field.

A subject field can be divided into several subfields. This breakdown of a field, which is discussed in further detail in Chapter 6, *SUBJECT-FIELD RESEARCH*, enables the terminologist to pinpoint the specific area of a field to which a term belongs. For example, the term *ratings* is used generally in broadcasting, more specifically in television production, even more specifically in audience measurement, and ultimately comes under audience research.

A single term can be used in several different fields, but the concept it covers changes in each one. *Carrier*, for example, is used in telecommunications to refer to a company involved in the transmission of telephone signals; in transportation to denote a company that transports goods or passengers by land, water or air; in insurance to designate a company that indemnifies for losses and provides monetary benefits, i.e. an insurance company; and in medicine to refer to someone who harbours and disseminates a microorganism or other agent causing an infectious disease to which he or she is immune.

For the terminologist, these terms are distinct because the concepts and realities they designate are distinct. Strictly speaking, a term belongs to a single subject field.

## 4.5 Object

The terms peculiar to any field—physics, medicine, biology, chemistry—serve to designate realities that can be tangible or intangible. *Object* must therefore be considered in the broadest sense and defined as encompassing any part of the perceivable or conceivable world. Objects can be material (e.g. computer) or immaterial (e.g. energy).[5]

From the earliest times, thinkers have sought to categorize objects into various classes in an effort to structure and order our knowledge of the world. The well-known Aristotelian categories, although somewhat expanded, are as follows:[6]

(a)    entities (material objects, immaterial objects and principles)
(b)    properties (quantities, relations and qualities)
(c)    activities (operations, processes, states)
(d)    dimensions (time, space, positions)

These categories are particularly useful in classifying the objects of terminological research and in describing or defining their concepts.

## 4.6    Relationship between Term and Concept

The relationship between word and idea has always been central to speculation on language origin. Swiss linguist Ferdinand de Saussure claimed that the linguistic sign is arbitrary. In other words, the signifier is arbitrary in relation to the signified; there is no natural or inherent connection between word and meaning. The relationship between them is based strictly on convention.[7] The same can be said of term and concept.

Scholars agree that there is no intrinsic reason for *bellis perennis* to be called *daisy* in English, or conversely for the

---

5. CSA Standard CAN/CSA-Z781-92. *Terminology—Vocabulary*, 2.1, p. 1.

6. Different authors have developed various classifications, but they all appear to be based on the Aristotelian categories. This particular categorization is provided by Ingetraut Dahlbert in "Terminological Definitions: Characteristics and Demands," in *Problèmes de la définition et de la synonymie en terminologie* (Québec: GIRSTERM, 1983), pp. 25–26.

7. S. Ullmann, *Semantics*, pp. 83–84.

English term *daisy* to denote *bellis perennis* and not something else. The conventionality of the relationship between term and concept is reflected in the fact that (a) a single term can represent two or more concepts (polysemy), and (b) two or more terms can represent the same concept (synonymy).

### 4.6.1 Motivation

While there is no natural connection between term and concept, a term can nonetheless be motivated. A term is considered to be motivated when the morphemes it contains provide an idea of the concept it covers. *Film library*, for example, is motivated or transparent because the concept it represents—a place in which films are organized and kept for use—can be seen through its form. *Catwalk*, used in television production to designate a narrow walkway joining the upper levels of a television studio, is less motivated than *film library*, but is still suggestive of the concept it represents through analogy. *Soap opera* is unmotivated or opaque because there is nothing in its form that is indicative or suggestive of the concept.

The motivation of a term is useful but not necessary. A large number of terms that are not motivated or that have lost their motivation, e.g. *blackboard*, which can be green or any dark colour, function very well as elements of discourse. The relationship between a term and a concept is ensured by a stable, well-established convention.

In special languages, motivation is considered desirable in newly created terms. Many experts believe that, to be adequate and accurate, a term should reflect an essential characteristic of the concept. Their efforts are directed at avoiding ambiguity and facilitating effective communication.

The motivation of a term can also prove valuable in concept classification, provided the established meaning of morphemes is respected, particularly in the case of forms borrowed from Latin and Greek. The way in which some terms are created appears to be totally haphazard. Take, for example, the combining form *path*, which is used in the formation of numerous medical terms. It comes from the Greek *pathos*, which means suffering. In some cases, it is used to refer to someone who suffers from a disease, such as in *psychopath*, and in other cases to designate someone who administers treatment, such as in *naturopath* or *homeopath*.

Ultimately, motivation helps strengthen the relationship between term and concept by making it less arbitrary.

### 4.6.2 Monosemy or Polysemy

According to some schools of thought, a term should represent only one concept. This is referred to as *monosemy*. Living language does not, however, follow such rigid lines. What's more, the number of stems and affixes in a language which can be used in the formation of terms is small in relation to the number of concepts in each subject field.[8] Thus monosemy is impractical and unachievable in any strict sense.

As a result, *polysemy*, where one term represents two or more concepts, is a natural characteristic of special languages, but one that needs to be controlled. Special languages require clarity of communication. Polysemy within a subject field, or worse, within a subfield, can create considerable confusion.

Terminological work should therefore strive, insofar as possible, to discourage or eliminate polysemy within a special language. If polysemy cannot be eliminated, each concept represented by a term must be carefully delimited in order to clarify semantic boundaries.

### 4.6.3 Synonymy

Some schools of thought also believe that a concept should be designated by only one term. This is certainly far from

---

8. H. Felbert, *Terminology Manual*, p. 183.

the reality of special languages, as two or more terms are often used to designate the same concept.

There are numerous reasons for synonymy: parallel use of the inventor's name and an essential characteristic as elements of complex terms, e.g. *Likert scale* and *summated scale*; parallel use of a trade name and a specialized term, e.g. *aspirin* and *acetylsalicylic acid*; parallel use of regionalisms, e.g. *random sampling* and *probability sampling*, and so on.[9]

One of the problems with synonyms is that they give the appearance of representing different concepts. Thus the importance in terminological research of pinpointing all differences among synonyms. Chapter 12, *SYNONYMY*, discusses how synonyms are studied and differentiated in terminological work.

## 4.7 Classification of Concepts

The knowledge structure of a subject field is made up of concepts that are interrelated. These concepts acquire their full meaning through their relationship with other concepts. It is therefore essential to identify such relationships in order to determine the position a concept occupies in a given subject field or subfield.

### 4.7.1 Intrinsic Relationships

There are two types of intrinsic relationships among concepts: hierarchical and non-hierarchical.

Hierarchical relationships may be either generic or partitive. In a generic relationship, concept A encompasses and is broader than concept B. For example, *sampling* can include *unsystematic sampling*, which in turn can include *judgment sampling* and *quota sampling*. In a partitive relationship, concept A is the whole and concept B the parts. For example, *bicycle* is the whole, and *frame, fork, wheel, pedal, saddle*, etc. are the parts.

---

9. *Ibid.*, p. 185.

Non-hierarchical relationships include causal connections, e.g. *biased sampling* (cause) and *biased results* (effect), and oppositional relationships, e.g. *systematic sampling* versus *unsystematic sampling*.

### 4.7.2 Extrinsic Relationships

In practice, the concepts of a subject field can be categorized according to the methods with which that field operates. For example, if we wanted to categorize the concepts falling under audience measurement tools, we could do so under questionnaires, questions and attitude scales. This type of classification is particularly useful in preparing a subject field breakdown, which is discussed in Chapter 6, *SUBJECT-FIELD RESEARCH*.

## 4.8   Conclusion

Term and concept together form a unit. The relationship between them must be clear and unambiguous. Thus the need to study the terminology units that make up the nomenclature of a given field. Such study forms the basis of all terminological work.

# BIBLIOGRAPHY

CSA Standard CAN/CSA-Z780-92. *Principles and Methods of Terminology*. Toronto: Canadian Standards Association, June 1992.

CSA Standard CAN/CSA-Z781-92. *Terminology—Vocabulary*. Toronto: Canadian Standards Association, June 1992.

Felbert, Helmut. *Terminology Manual*. Paris: Unesco, 1984.

Nida, Eugene. *Componential Analysis of Meaning: An Introduction to Semantic Structures*. The Hague: Mouton & Co., 1975.

Palmer, F.R. *Semantics*. 2nd ed. Cambridge, England: Cambridge University Press, 1981.

Sager, Juan C. *A Practical Course in Terminology Processing*. Philadelphia: John Benjamins Publishing Company, 1990.

Ullmann, Stephen. *Semantics*. New York: Barnes & Noble, 1967.

# EXERCISES

1. Which is more important in terminology: term or concept? Discuss.

2. Why is terminological work concerned with *objects* as defined in this chapter?

3. To what extent are polysemy and synonymy undesirable in special languages? Discuss.

4. List five motivated terms used in a given subject and explain why they are motivated.

*Report on Chernobyl*

# CHAPTER 5

# TERM RESEARCH

## 5.0 Introduction

Terminological research that is conducted on individual terms or concepts is referred to as *term research*.[1] This type of research accounts for a significant part of the terminological work performed by private organizations and government agencies. It is intended to provide answers to the terminological questions of a wide variety of users, from the layman to the expert.

## 5.1 Advantages of Term Research

Some terminologists take exception to term research, viewing it as a type of piecemeal work that cannot really offer global solutions to the terminological requirements of the workplace. For them, isolated solutions that are not researched as part of a terminological system may or may not ultimately fit into that system.

Certainly there is a measure of truth to this. Term research is often a stopgap measure, but a necessary one that meets the wide-ranging terminology needs of the general public, language professional and subject specialist. Ideally, subject-field research would be carried out in every field of endeavour. But this would require time and money: two resources often at a premium. Even if these resources were readily available, subject-field research could never keep pace with developing fields of knowledge. There would always be new

---

[1]. In its *Vocabulary of Terminology* (Ottawa: Terminology Directorate, Secretary of State, 1983), the Secretary of State makes a distinction between *single-term research*, which is carried out on an **individual** term or concept, and *multiple-term research*, which is carried out on a **group** of terms or concepts specific to one or more subject fields.

concepts to be named, new problems to be solved, new users to be helped.

Term research is excellent training for the novice terminologist. It offers an opportunity to work directly with the user and thus gain insight into the user's needs and the peculiarities of each situation. Somehow, knowing that the term you have to locate is to go into the company president's speech—which he will be delivering at the annual meeting the next day—puts the task in perspective. An awareness of the situation is essential in all terminological work, and constitutes an effective safeguard against taking an overly theoretical approach.

Term research is a particularly instructive experience because of the conditions under which it is practised. Clients can ask questions on almost any topic and usually need an answer quickly (within 4 to 48 hours). As a result, term researchers sharpen their skills at assimilating information on various subjects, become thoroughly familiar with the documentation at their disposal, and develop a keen sense of which document is likely to contain a given answer.

## 5.2   Steps in Term Research

### 5.2.1   Discussion with the Client

The first step in term research is to ask the client to specify the concept, the field to which it belongs, the situation in which its designation will be used, the source-language term in the case of a bilingual question, and any measures he or she may have taken to find a solution. Not all clients are aware of what term research involves; some may feel inconvenienced or be taken aback by all these questions. So it is important to exercise tact when probing for information.

### 5.2.2   Checking the Concept

The next step is to verify the information the client has supplied. If the client is working between two languages and has provided the source-language term, the term and its definition should be checked in general or specialized source-language dictionaries. This enables the terminologist to supplement the sometimes scant information provided by the client or detect any discrepancies between the client's explanation and the dictionary definition.

### 5.2.3 Consulting a Specialist

Consulting a specialist at this stage can be particularly helpful. If the terminologist does not know the source-language term, the specialist can confirm the concept, provide further useful information, and suggest sources in which the term may be found. If the terminologist *does* know the source-language term and has found discrepancies between the client's explanation and the dictionary definition, the specialist can usually provide clarification, and thus help keep the research on track.

### 5.2.4 Researching the Solution

Once the terminologist has an adequate understanding of the concept, he or she can begin to look for the appropriate expression. In the case of monolingual research, the basic characteristics[2] of the concept should be analyzed to determine which dictionary or encyclopedia entry, or section of a reference work, is most likely to deal with the subject.

For example, someone from the marine security division of a watercraft manufacturer is writing an accident report and needs to know what the rotating light on a lighthouse is called. The concept may be analyzed as follows:

| | |
|---|---|
| Field: | navigation |
| Nature: | light |
| Character: | rotating |
| Location: | lighthouse |
| Purpose: | marine security |

---

2. The properties that describe the object (see Chapter 4, section 4.5) to which a concept refers, i.e. nature, function, material, shape, etc.

These characteristics are points of reference which can be used to track down the name of the light in general dictionaries, encyclopedias, or specialized works on the subject. Let's consider the possibilities. This type of light is only one of many lighting devices used in navigation, but it is a major component of a lighthouse. Thus, the logical place to begin is under *lighthouse* in the encyclopedia. This entry provides a brief treatment of *lighthouse* and refers the reader to *Public Works*, which includes a section on lighthouses and their illuminants, and contains the answer to the question: *flashing light*.

In the case of bilingual research, the terminologist should look up the source-language term in the organization's terminology database and outside term banks, as well as in bilingual dictionaries, vocabularies or glossaries on the subject. If these bilingual sources do not provide any answers, the procedure recommended for monolingual research should be followed.

### 5.2.5 Checking the Solution

Before the client is given a solution which has been found in bilingual terminological or lexicographic sources, it should be checked in monolingual works to make sure it represents the concept in question. If the works consulted do not confirm that the term found covers the concept, a specialist can always be consulted. Once the term has been checked and its suitability determined, the solution can be given to the client.

### 5.2.6 Presenting the Solution

When presenting the research findings to the client, the terminologist should be prepared to justify the solution, name the source in which it was found, establish the credibility of the specialist consulted, and offer any other relevant information.

If the research proves inconclusive, a solution can be suggested through analogy with similar situations.

For example, a translator working on a text describing the many and varied advantages of buying tomorrow's telephone system today comes up against the expression *coupure d'appel en attente*. This function enables the telephone user to eliminate the call waiting tone during selected phone calls.

No English equivalent can be located for the term. However, there are a number of other functions based on the same principle, such as *coupure de sonnerie* (*ringing disable*) and *coupure sélective de sonnerie* (*selective ringing disable*). Since *coupure* is rendered in these expressions as *disable*, and since *call waiting tone* is an established term in telecommunications parlance, it would be possible to suggest *call waiting tone disable* to the translator as an equivalent to the elliptical expression *coupure d'appel en attente*.[3] It is important, however, to stress to the client that this is merely a suggestion and not a documented solution.

## 5.3 Why Consult General Works, then Specialized?

In term research, it is advisable to consult general documentation first, then more specialized. This is primarily because of the time constraints imposed on term research and because of the availability of specialized documentation. General dictionaries and encyclopedias are intended for the public at large, and are thus quicker and easier to consult. They provide all the meanings of each headword and often give an overview of the concept, which can help orient the research. They do not, however, offer the same level of technical detail or rigour as specialized material, a fact which must be taken into account when checking the concept.

---

3. Strictly speaking, this is a question of term formation, which is the subject of Chapter 13.

Obviously, terminologists need not consult general works if they know a particular specialized text contains the answer they are looking for. With experience, term researchers become so familiar with their documentation that they know precisely where to look for a given answer. For the novice, it is advisable to follow the approach outlined in this chapter.

## BIBLIOGRAPHY

Brunette, Louise and Tina Célestin. *Compte rendu des rencontres sur la recherche ponctuelle en terminologie*. Québec: Office de la langue française, 1979.

Célestin, Tina et al. *Méthodologie de la recherche terminologique ponctuelle, Essai de définition*. Québec: Office de la langue française, 1984.

## EXERCISES

1. Situation:

    A food manufacturer has just perfected a new product which contains *tofu*. The manufacturer is adamant about not listing *tofu* as one of the ingredients in case people question the taste or texture of his innovation. He maintains that *bean curd* is the same thing as *tofu*, and wants to list *bean curd* as one of the ingredients.

    Question:

    Is *bean curd*, in fact, the same as *tofu*? Once you have researched the question, describe the approach you took—the sources you consulted, the order in which you consulted them, etc.—as well as your conclusions.

2. Situation:

   Another food manufacturer is about to market an easy-to-cook breakfast cereal containing whole oats, long-grain brown rice, rye, hard red winter wheat, triticale, raw buckwheat, barley, and mechanically dehulled sesame seeds. The product is cooked in water, broth or other liquid, in similar proportions and in a similar manner to rice. The manufacturer would like to call the product a *breakfast pilaf*.

   Question:

   Is *breakfast pilaf* an appropriate name for such a product? Research the question and outline your findings.

3. Context:

   Over the course of a few months, a translator comes across the French terms *globalisation* and *décloisonnement* a number of times. Suddenly, it seems, various sectors of the economy—insurance, financial services, etc.—are all discussing how we have resolutely entered the age of *globalisation* and *décloisonnement*, how the *globalisation* and *décloisonnement* of financial services, for example, will open the door to many new markets and, at the same time, give rise to fierce competition.

   Question: *fragmentalizacion*

   What exactly do these expressions mean? What are their English equivalents?

4. Context:

   *Rollout* has become quite a popular expression. Marketing experts talk about the *rollout* of a new product with an unmistakable sense of expectancy. Telecommunications experts discuss the *rollout* of new technology in the broadest terms imaginable. Precisely what they mean remains somewhat ill-defined, even by them. They seem to be using the term to refer to the entire implementation process for new technology, from the planning and acquisition phases through to installation and user training.

Question:

Are these logical uses of the term? Research and discuss.

# CHAPTER 6

# SUBJECT-FIELD RESEARCH

## 6.0 Introduction

Terminological research that is carried out on the terms and concepts specific to a given subject or field of knowledge is referred to as *subject-field research*. This type of research is relatively exhaustive and generally conducted over a fairly long period. As a result, the terminologist must take a thorough and systematic approach to it.

## 6.1 Stages of Subject-Field Research

There are a number of preliminary stages involved in subject-field research which must be completed before the terminologist can begin to scan for and extract terms. These stages include determining research objectives; estimating the necessary resources; becoming familiar with the subject field; selecting and evaluating the documentation; and preparing a breakdown of the subject field.

### 6.1.1 Determining the Objectives

The starting point of any subject-field work is to determine the **purpose, target audience** and **scope** of the research in conjunction with the client. These considerations are vital, as they will influence the entire orientation of the work.

The **purpose** of subject-field research will differ with each client, and can vary from filling a total gap to revising and enlarging existing material. The **target audience** can range from the layman to the specialist, or include just about any group in between: company manager, language professional or subject enthusiast.

The **scope** of the research will depend on the client's needs. If the client needs the basic terminology of a field, a terminological work (vocabulary or glossary) containing a few hundred concepts would likely be sufficient. If the client needs the complete terminology of a field or major subfield, a work containing a few thousand concepts would be more appropriate.

Consider the following example. A few years ago the research department of a broadcasting corporation commissioned terminological research on audience measurement. Broadcast technology had been changing at a tremendous pace and with it the nature and composition of the audience; broadcast researchers had been developing new techniques in an effort to survey and measure increasingly elusive television and radio audiences.

These changes naturally had a significant effect on the terminology of audience research. A host of new terms had entered the vocabulary of researchers. However, the precise meaning of some terms created spontaneously in the field was as vague as the usage of other terms borrowed from related disciplines, such as the behavioural sciences. Dictionaries in related fields were no longer meeting the needs of audience measurement as it evolved and expanded.

When the research department approached the corporation's terminology division about compiling a French-English, English-French vocabulary of audience measurement terms within a one-year period, the **purpose, target audience** and **scope** of the undertaking were clear: to provide all those involved in audience research—managers, researchers, and support staff—with a vocabulary of the terms that describe the entire measurement process and underlying principles.

### 6.1.2 Estimating the Resources

The **human, documentary** and **financial resources** needed to carry out the work must also be discussed with the client and the following questions given due consideration. **Human resources**: How many terminologists are needed to conduct the research? Is support staff available to key in terminological data? Are one or more subject-field specialists able to participate in the various stages of the work? **Documentary resources**: Are original documents (not translations) available in the source and target languages? Are vocabularies or glossaries available in the subject field or in related fields? Are computerized bibliographic databases accessible? Do terminology banks contain material on the subject field? **Financial resources**: What are the financial resources required? Are sufficient funds available?

After the terminologist and client have determined the human and documentary resources needed for the project, a quote specifying the various costs should be drawn up for client approval. The quote should provide a breakdown of the costs of acquiring the documentation, the number of person-hours required for the various stages of the work—terminologists, specialists and support staff—and the cost of preparing the finished product.

### 6.1.3  Becoming Familiar with the Field

Once the research objectives have been established and the resources allocated, the terminologist must become familiar with the subject field. One of the best ways of doing so is to read a concise work on the subject, intended for the uninitiate. This type of work will provide an overview of the subject, indicate its knowledge structure, and discuss the basic concepts to be investigated during the research proper. General reference works which treat the subject as a whole, such as introductory textbooks, encyclopedia entries and general articles, are also very useful.

If the scanning process is automated, the terminologist will need more time to become familiar with the field, as there will not be an opportunity to do so through manual scanning. This step is crucial, as the terminologist must have an adequate knowledge of the field in order to grasp the concepts and determine where they fit into it.

During this stage in the research process, it is advisable to examine the bibliographies of all works consulted and note any pertinent sources that seem worth including in the research documentation.

### 6.1.4 Selecting the Documentation

The quality of the terminology researched depends on the quality of the documentation from which it is extracted. Thus, the quality of documents and their relevance to the research are more important than the quantity. For monolingual subject-field research, three or four basic works and a specialized dictionary should enable the terminologist to meet the research objectives quite adequately, even if it means consulting supplementary sources to fill in any gaps.

This guideline also applies to bilingual subject-field research. Three or four basic works in the source language should enable the terminologist to gather most of the source-language terminology. More works are needed in the target language, since the concepts of a field are often classified differently from one language to another. Six or eight carefully selected works should be sufficient for locating most of the target-language equivalents. Secondary works—specialized source- and target-language dictionaries, and specialized bilingual dictionaries, vocabularies and glossaries—may be useful for checking information.

### 6.1.4.1 Locating the Documentation

The research documentation can include textbooks, handbooks and standards published by national standards associations like the CSA (Canada Standards Association) and ASTM (American Society for Testing and Materials). Documents can be tracked down through manual or automated bibliographies at public, corporate or university libraries, ordered from publishers, or acquired from specialized bookstores. The assistance of documentalists, librarians and subject-field specialists can prove invaluable. Documentalists and librarians can query bibliographic databases as well as locate and acquire documentation; subject-field specialists can indicate the latest sources, provide inside information on unpublished reports and working papers, and single out the most authoritative publications in each subfield.

### 6.1.4.2 Evaluating the Documentation

There are a number of generally accepted guidelines to be considered in evaluating the suitability and quality of documentation. To determine the suitability of each work, the terminologist should check the table of contents and index, and look up different sections to <u>assess how well the concepts are explained</u> and <u>how relevant they are to the research subject</u>. To determine the quality, the terminologist should evaluate the quality of the writing, the credibility of the author, and the importance of the work in the subject field. <u>The documents ultimately selected</u> must be <u>original-language documents</u>, not translations, and should include works from <u>the main geographic areas</u> in which the source and target languages are spoken.

### 6.1.5 Preparing a Breakdown of the Subject Field

*[margin note: Can you break down your subject field?]*

Once the research documents have been selected, the terminologist should take a close look at them to study the structure of the subject and to prepare a breakdown of the field. This involves dividing the subject field into subfields and identifying any related fields the research may touch upon.

The breakdown is not intended to provide a scientific classification of the concepts involved, but rather a functional means of categorizing the terms and concepts researched. In preparing the breakdown, the terminologist should determine both the general subjects under which the research subject falls and the main subfields into which the research subject can be divided. Thus, <u>the breakdown includes two parts: the first places the research subject in the broader fields of which it is a part; the second</u> serves to structure the research, and categorize the concepts according to their intrinsic or extrinsic relationships (see Chapter 4, *TERM AND CONCEPT*, sections 4.7.1 and 4.7.2).

A subject-field breakdown for audience measurement, for example, would include the following two parts. The first shows the general fields to which the research subject belongs:

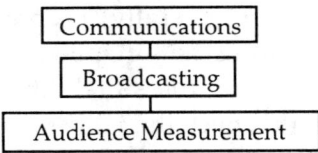

The second divides the research subject into subfields:

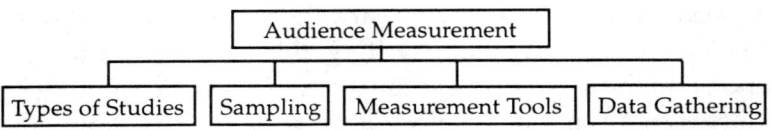

Only the lower three levels of the breakdown—broadcasting, audience measurement, and the appropriate subfield, e.g. types of studies, sampling, or measurement tools, as the case may be—need to be indicated on the terminology record.

The actual scope of a subject field becomes clear only after close study. As the research progresses, the terminologist may need to adjust the breakdown, eliminating some subfields that prove to be of little importance and adding others that prove useful.

There is no hard-and-fast rule on how to subdivide a field. Each field has its own particular structure which may be broken down in more than one way. In a word, a subject-field breakdown is essential because it provides a structure for the research and an overview of the work.

### 6.1.6 Scanning for Terms

The main objective of scanning the selected documentation is to identify the terms and concepts specific to the research subject. Each terminology unit identified must fit into the subject-field breakdown; if it does not, it should be considered irrelevant and be disregarded. In the initial stages of scanning, it may be questionable as to whether some of the terms identified are actually relevant. Generally speaking, it is wiser to include too many terms at the beginning than not enough. There will always be time during the research process to eliminate any terms that are unsuitable.

## 6.2 Conclusion

Subject-field research is comparable to bicycle touring and many other long-distance activities. It serves little purpose to jump on any old bicycle and charge through the countryside at top speed. In bicycle touring, as in subject-field research, it is important to know precisely where you are going, to map out the route, and to be properly equipped.

# EXERCISE

✓ Prepare a breakdown for the subject of **Coffee** using the following text:

**COFFEE**

Coffee, a beverage brewed from the roasted and ground seeds of the tropical evergreen coffee plant of African origin, is consumed either hot or cold by about one third of the people in the world, in amounts larger than those of any other drink. Its popularity can be attributed to its invigorating effect, which is produced by caffeine, an alkaloid present in green coffee in amounts between 0.8 and 1.5 percent for the Arabica species, and 1.6 to 2.5 percent for the Robusta species. Because of its caffeine and other alkaloids, coffee has physiological effects, particularly on the nervous and circulatory systems. It stimulates cerebral and cardiac activity, and functions as a diuretic. Coffee or caffeine may be prescribed in the treatment of certain cases of heart disease, dropsy, migraine, chronic asthma, and barbiturate poisoning. Excessive amounts may produce excessive gastric acidity, nervousness, and heightened cardiac action. Fatal results from overdoses of coffee or caffeine have never been reported in humans but can be demonstrated in laboratory animals.

## HISTORY

Wild coffee plants, probably from Kefa (Kaffa), Ethiopia, were taken to southern Arabia and placed under cultivation in the 15th century. One of many legends about the discovery of coffee is that of Kaldi, an Arab goatherd, who was puzzled by the queer antics of his flock. About AD 850, Kaldi supposedly sampled the berries of the evergreen bush on which the goats were feeding and, on experiencing a sense of exhilaration, proclaimed his discovery to the world.

Whatever its historical origin, the stimulating effect of coffee undoubtedly made it popular, especially in connection with the long religious service of the Muslims. The orthodox priesthood pronounced it intoxicating and therefore prohibited by the Quran, but despite the threat of severe penalties, coffee drinking spread rapidly among Arabs and their neighbours.

During the 16th and 17th centuries, coffee was introduced into one European country after another; many accounts are recorded of its prohibition or approval as a religious, political, and medical potion. Coffee gained popularity as a beverage in the coffeehouses of London, which became centres of political, social, literary, and eventually business influence. The first London coffeehouse was established about 1652. In Europe, too, the coffeehouse flourished later in the 17th century. In such North American cities as Boston, New York City, and Philadelphia, coffeehouses became popular starting about 1689.

Until the close of the 17th century, the world's limited supply of coffee was obtained almost entirely from the province of Yemen in southern Arabia. But, with the increasing popularity of the beverage, the propagation of the plant spread rapidly to Ceylon in 1658, Java and other islands of the Indonesian archipelago starting about 1696, Haiti and Santo Domingo 1715, Surinam 1718, Martinique 1723, Brazil 1727, Jamaica 1730, Cuba 1748, Puerto Rico 1755, Costa Rica 1779, Venezuela 1784, Mexico 1790, Colombia late 18th century, and El Salvador 1840. Coffee cultivation was started in the Hawaiian Islands in 1825.

By the 20th century, coffee had become responsible for much of the income of many countries lying between the Tropic of Capricorn and the Tropic of Cancer. Although practically every country within this area produces some coffee, the greatest concentration of production is centred in the Western Hemisphere. This situation changed somewhat, however, toward the mid-20th century as the growth of coffee in Africa began to assume importance.

POST-HARVEST HANDLING

**Processing.** The ripened fruits of the coffee shrubs, known as coffee cherries, are processed by disengaging the coffee seeds from their coverings and from the pulp. Two different techniques are used: a wet process and a dry process.

*The wet process.* First the fresh fruit is pulped by a pulping machine. Some pulp still clings to the coffee, however, and this residue, a mucilaginous substance, is eliminated by fermentation in tanks, which brings about a decomposition of pectic substances in 18 to 36 hours. Washing clears all remaining traces of pulp from the coffee seeds, which are then dried to a moisture content of about 12 percent either by exposure to the sun or by hot-air driers. The mechanical operation that follows removes the seed parchment, the endocarp, and also the pellicle more or less completely, sometimes with polishing.

*The dry process.* In the dry process, the fruits are immediately placed to dry either in the sun or in hot-air driers. More time and equipment are required for drying than in the wet process. When the fruits have been dried to a water content of 12 percent, they are mechanically hulled to free the seeds from their coverings.

**Grading and storage.** The practice of grading coffee gives sellers and buyers a guarantee concerning the origin, nature, and quality of the product to aid their negotiations. Each country has a certain number of defined types and grades, but there are no international standards outside the contract market.

The prolonged storage of coffee in the producing countries may present problems, especially in the warm and humid coastal regions, where molds and parasites may develop and cause damage; for this reason coffee from these areas is exported as quickly as possible. In moderate climates, the conservation of dry lots does not pose a problem as long as they are stocked in well-ventilated places.

MANUFACTURE OF COFFEE PRODUCTS

**Roasting.** The aromatic and gustatory qualities of coffee only appear in and are developed by the high temperatures to which they are subjected during the course of a process called either roasting or broiling.

Temperatures are raised progressively to about 430–440°F (220–230°C). This releases steam, carbon dioxide, carbon monoxide, and other volatiles from the beans, resulting in a loss of weight between 14 and 23 percent. Internal pressure of gas expands the coffee seeds volumetrically from 30 to 100 percent. The seeds become deep, rich brown in colour; their texture becomes porous and crumbly under pressure. But the most important phenomenon of roasting is the appearance of the characteristic aroma of coffee, which arises from very complex chemical transformations within the bean.

In the most common method for roasting, hot air is propelled by a blower into a metal cylinder containing the coffee. In another technique, called singeing, the seed is submitted to the direct action of a flame. In the latter method, which is older, a metal cylinder, or sphere, containing the coffee is rotated above a source of heat such as charcoal, gas, or electricity.

Regardless of the method used, the coffee, after leaving the industrial roasters, is rapidly cooled in a vat, where it is stirred and subjected to cold air propelled by a blower. Good-quality coffees are then sorted by electronic sorters to eliminate those seeds, either too light or too dark, that roasted badly, and whose presence depreciates the quality.

**Grinding.** Some coffees are left as whole beans to be ground at the time of purchase or by the consumer at home. But a large part of the coffee is ground, or milled, by the manufacturer immediately after roasting. There are special types of mills for the dripolator, percolator, expresso, and other methods of brewing. The degree of fineness is important; if a coffee is too coarse, water filters through too fast to pick up enough aroma; if a coffee is too fine, water filters through too slowly and retains small particles that deposit at the bottom of the cup.

**Packaging.** Effective packaging prevents air from reaching the coffee. Ground coffee alters rapidly and loses its aromatic qualities if it is not put into hermetically sealed containers immediately.

The air, especially in humid atmospheres, causes rancidity through oxidation of fatty components. Modern packaging materials, plastic films like polyethylene and complexes of aluminum and cellulose, are capable of conserving the quality of coffee for a time. But the most satisfactory solution to the problem is packing under vacuum or in an inert gas, in rigorously impervious containers.

**Types of coffee.** *Soluble coffee.* In the manufacture of soluble coffee, a liquid concentration of coffee prepared with hot water is dehydrated. This can be done by spray drying in hot air, by drying under vacuum, or by lyophilization (freeze-drying). The operations are complex and methods vary among manufacturers. The resulting soluble powder, on the addition of hot water, forms reconstituted coffee. The average yield is 25 to 30 percent by weight of the ground coffee.

Because it picks up moisture readily, soluble coffee needs special vacuum packages.

*Decaffeinated coffee.* Caffeine may be freed from green coffee by the action of acids, alkalis, hot water, or steam; it may be extracted using a chlorinated solvent such as dichloroethylene or trichloroethylene. The coffee is then roasted. The caffeine content of decaffeinated coffees is often regulated by law. In France, for example, caffeine content must be less than 0.1 percent by weight.

*Coffee substitutes.* Of many substitutes for coffee, the most popular is the roasted and ground root of the chicory plant, *Cichorium intybus*, used mainly in Belgium, the Netherlands, Germany, and India. Chicory is also used in some areas to flavour or to adulterate coffee.

Certain cereal grains, particularly barley, and leguminous seeds, such as lupin and soya, are sometimes roasted and used as a coffee substitute.

Source: *The New Encyclopaedia Britannica*, Volume 14 (Chicago: Encyclopaedia Britannica, Inc., 1987).

# CHAPTER 7

# TERMINOLOGICAL ANALYSIS

## 7.0 Introduction

Terminological analysis is central to the subject-field research process. It involves identifying the terms specific to the field of study and analyzing the contexts in which they appear.

## 7.1 Identification of Terms

A term or terminology unit is the name or designation of a concept specific to a subject field. As discussed in Chapter 1, section 1.2.2.1, the terminology of a given field includes all means of expression peculiar to that field: simple terms, complex terms and terminological phrases.

There are a number of factors to be taken into account when identifying terminology units. They include the relationship between the determinant[1] and determinatum,[2] degree of lexicalization, classification of concepts, collocation and typographic indications.

### 7.1.1 Relationship between Determinant and Determinatum

Analyzing the relationship between determinant and determinatum is essential in identifying a terminology unit. Only those determinants that fundamentally modify the determinatum are considered part of a terminology unit. Thus, it is important to distinguish essential determinants

---

1. In complex terminology units, the element that qualifies the meaning of the base word or *determinatum*, e.g. *desktop* in *desktop publishing* or *double-sided* and *double-density* in *double-sided double-density diskette*.

2. In complex terminology units, the base word that is qualified by the *determinant*, e.g. *advertising* in *subliminal advertising* and *editing* in *film editing*.

from inessential. This is not always clear-cut, since the same determinant can be essential in some cases and inessential in others. Take *charitable*, for example, in the expressions *charitable institution* and *charitable man*. In the first case, *charitable* is essential because it defines the type of institution—an institution engaged in relief of the poor—and differentiates it from others, e.g. *educational institution*; in the second case, *charitable* is circumstantial because it refers to an attribute, i.e. benevolent or generous, observable in an individual. Establishing whether a determinant is essential or inessential requires a thorough analysis of the concept in question and of its place in the conceptual framework of the subject field.

### 7.1.1.1 Inessential Determinants

Inessential determinants modify the determinatum, without substantially changing its meaning. For example, in the expression *intricate technology product*, *intricate* simply refers to complexity, but does not fundamentally alter the meaning of *technology product*. *Initial* in the expression *initial verification technique* simply refers to the first in a series, but does not significantly change the meaning of *verification technique*. *Intricate* and *initial* are inessential determinants and should not be included in the terminology units *technology product* and *verification technique*.

### 7.1.1.2 Essential Determinants

Essential determinants specify a vital aspect of the determinatum. Take, for example, the following advertising terms which reflect only two of the countless ingenious ways devised to influence our thinking and behaviour: *bait-and-switch advertising* and *advocacy advertising*. In *bait-and-switch advertising*, store owners advertise a product at a low price to lure the consumer into the store, deliberately carry very little of the product so it is usually out of stock early in the sale period, and hope the consumer will buy a similar product at full price. In *advocacy advertising*, an editorial message promoting a particular point of view on an issue of public interest is published in the print media. *Bait-and-switch* and *advocacy* are essential determinants as they differentiate the types of advertising and specify their purpose. As a result, they should be included in the terminology units.

### 7.1.2 Degree of Lexicalization

Terminology units are sometimes less lexicalized[3] than lexical units.[4] There are two basic reasons for this. First, terminology units are considered part of spoken or written messages; various forms of a term may be used in context. One form is often less lexicalized than the others. For example, the author of an article on network environments may vary his terms and speak of *security of networks, network security* or simply *security*. Second, the terminology of many developing fields is usually evolving. As a result, terminology units are not as set as lexical units, thus the appearance of more or less lexicalized variants.[5] For example, the same article on network environments is just as apt to refer to *validation in real time* as *real-time validation*. These variants are important to note, as they indicate the forms of expression that are used in context.

As a guideline, it is useful to bear in mind that highly lexicalized terms representing a precise concept in a given field are almost invariably terminology units. However, a low degree of lexicalization does not necessarily preclude an expression from being a terminology unit.

### 7.1.3 Classification of Concepts

The terminologist ultimately decides whether a particular expression is in fact a terminology unit by referring to the

---

3. A highly lexicalized term is one composed primarily of closely linked lexical or vocabulary items and is characterized by the absence of linking function words, i.e. articles, conjunctions, prepositions.

4. A unit of the vocabulary of a language, such as a word or phrase listed in a dictionary.

5. See Chapter 12, *SYNONYMY*, section 12.1 for a full explanation of variants.

conceptual framework of the subject field. For example, in the field of audience measurement (see Chapter 6, *SUBJECT-FIELD RESEARCH*, section 6.1.5), *unsystematic sampling* is a terminology unit because it is **opposed to** *systematic sampling; cluster sampling, area sampling* and *stratified sampling* are terminology units because they are **types** of systematic sampling. Thus, terminology units are identified in relation to other terminology units and the concepts they represent.[6] In all these cases, the determinants are essential as they serve to specify the relationships in question.

### 7.1.4 Collocation

A collocation or co-occurring expression is made up of two or more terms which typically appear in combination in a particular field. *To acknowledge receipt of a message, to clear a buffer* and *to formulate a query* are examples of collocations in the field of telematics. Collocations are not always verbal phrases but can be other parts of speech, e.g. *request for copyright clearance*, which is a nominal phrase. Collocated terms are considered to be terminology units because they are subject-specific expressions which frequently occur together.

### 7.1.5 Typographic Indications

The terminologist should also note the typographic devices used by an author: bold print, italics, quotation marks and underlining. These devices are often used to emphasize the

---

6. CSA Standard CAN/CSA-Z780-92, *Principles and Methods of Terminology* (Toronto: Canadian Standards Association, June 1992), identifies two types of relationships among concepts: hierarchical, which includes generic and partitive, and non-hierarchical. The relationship between *systematic sampling* and its various types is a generic one: *systematic sampling* represents the broader concept and the types represent the narrower concepts. The relationship between *loom*, found in the text in Chapter 8, and its components is a partitive one: *loom* is the whole and its components are the parts. The relationship between *first-phase sample* and *second-phase sample* is a non-hierarchical one, as the two concepts are part of the same process.

fundamental concepts of a field, and can sometimes mark a terminology unit.

## 7.2 Contextual Analysis

Once a term has been identified, the context in which it is found must be analyzed to determine the concept it represents and establish whether it belongs to the research subject. This step is also useful in detecting synonyms and variants, and in selecting the context to be entered on the terminology record.

### 7.2.1 Identification of Semantic Features

When analyzing the context in which a term appears, the terminologist must pinpoint the semantic features it contains. The most significant semantic features are those which describe the nature of a concept or object, its purpose, function, composition, material, cause or effect. Semantic features describing the dimensions, shape or use of an object are also important.

### 7.2.2 Context Selection

When selecting the context that will be entered on a terminology record to illustrate the meaning and use of a term, the terminologist must take into account the descriptive elements it contains. The space reserved for the context on records is limited so it is wise to select the most important semantic features, and to shorten the context to remove irrelevant information.

### 7.2.3 Types of Contexts

A context is called *defining*, *explanatory* or *associative* depending on the quality and quantity of semantic features it contains.

### 7.2.3.1 Defining Context

A defining context contains the term and sufficient semantic features to provide a clear idea of its meaning. It does not necessarily constitute a formal definition. The following is an example of a defining context for *weaving*: "Weaving is a method of producing cloth by interlacing two or more sets of yarns . . . at right angles to each other."[7] This context provides certain essential characteristics of the concept, i.e. the nature (method), the purpose (producing cloth), and the means by which it is achieved (interlacing . . . sets of yarns at right angles).

### 7.2.3.2 Explanatory Context

An explanatory context describes some characteristics of a concept, without necessarily defining it. The following is an example of an explanatory context for the term *shed*, which is used in weaving: "Each warp yarn must run straight from cloth beam to warp beam without being crossed with any other yarn; this is essential for raising and lowering the different harnesses to form a shed." This context explains how a shed is formed, without actually specifying its nature or function. For anyone with an understanding of how a loom works, it is clear that *shed* refers to the space created when the warp yarn is separated into two layers, although this is not explicitly stated in the context.

### 7.2.3.3 Associative Context

An associative context does not contain any semantic features. It simply enables the terminologist to link a term to the subject field through its association with the terms around it. Associative contexts are often found in texts written for learned or expert audiences who have a prior knowledge of the subject. The defining context for *weaving* above offers an

---

7. Evelyn E. Stout, *Introduction to Textiles*, 3rd ed. (New York: John Wiley and Sons, 1970), p. 317.

associative context for *yarn*. The only information the context offers is that yarn is used in the weaving process.

An associative context should not be used on a final terminology record, as it does not provide sufficient information on a concept to establish equivalence between source- and target-language designations.

## 7.3 Conclusion

In identifying terminology units, it is important to examine the relationship between the determinant and determinatum, to bear in mind that terminology units can be less lexicalized than lexical units, and to be on the look-out for co-occurring expressions. In analyzing the contexts in which terminology units appear, it is essential to zero in on the semantic features that best describe the concept. Term identification and contextual analysis together form the cornerstone of all terminological analysis.

## EXERCISES

1. Identify all the terminology units in the text on coffee found at the end of Chapter 6.

2. Select the context of 10 of the terminology units identified and pinpoint the semantic features they contain. Be sure to specify the type of context in each case.

# CHAPTER 8

# SAMPLE TERMINOLOGICAL ANALYSIS

## 8.0 Introduction

To illustrate the method of terminological analysis described in the preceding chapter, the terms appearing in the following text will be identified and commented on. The contexts in which they appear will then be selected, analyzed, and categorized according to type, i.e. defining, explanatory or associative.

WEAVING  *explanatory*

Weaving is a method of producing cloth by interlacing two or more sets of yarns, at least one warp and one filling set, at right angles to each other. The *warp* is also called *ends*, and the *filling* is also called *picks*, or *weft*. The warp runs from front to back of the loom and lengthwise in a woven fabric. Extra warp yarns at each side form a *selvage* during weaving. Filling yarns run across from side to side, or from selvage to selvage.

The machine for weaving is a *loom*, of which there are several types, varying in complexity. All looms, from the most primitive to the most modern, operate on similar principles . . . .

Essential parts of the loom include the *warp beam*, on which the warp yarns are wound; the *cloth beam*, on which the cloth is wound as it is woven; *harness frames* which carry the heddles, and which move up or down to form the weaving shed; *heddles*, each with an eye in the center, through which the individual yarns are threaded, usually one yarn to a heddle; the *reed*, which keeps the warp yarns separated, helps to determine cloth width, and acts as a beater; and *shuttles* or *bobbins* for carrying the filling yarns across from side to side.

In preparation for weaving, the warp yarns are measured and wound evenly on the warp beam according to the number of warp yarns needed for the entire width of fabric. Each warp yarn, in consecutive order, is drawn through the eye of the correct heddle on the correct harness frame, according to the pattern to be woven, and then is carried through the correct opening in the reed to the front of the loom where all the warp yarns, when the threading is completed, are evenly tensioned and tied to the cloth beam apron. Each warp yarn must run straight from cloth beam to warp beam without being crossed with any other yarn; this is essential for raising and lowering the different harnesses to form a *shed*. During weaving, the harnesses are raised and lowered in an order determined by the pattern; as one harness (or group of harnesses) is raised, the other (or others) is lowered, causing a separation of the warp yarns as the heddles are carried up or down with the frames, thus forming a shed. The shuttle carrying the filling yarn goes through the shed from one side to the other, and the yarn left by its passing is beaten forward by the reed against the tied-in knots at the cloth apron or against cloth already woven. The harnesses then change position, a new shed is formed, and the procedure is repeated over and over.[1]

## 8.1  Detection of Terms

The terminology units detected in the text above are as follows:

—*weaving* (Basic concept in the production of woven fabric.)

—*producing cloth* (to produce cloth) (Basic concept in the production of woven fabric.)

—*interlacing sets of yarn*s (to interlace sets of yarn) (Co-occurring expression which is broken down below.)

—*interlacing* (to interlace) (Basic concept in the production of woven fabric.)

—*set of yarn* (Basic concept in the production of woven fabric.)

—*yarn* (Basic concept in the production of woven fabric.)

---

1. Evelyn E. Stout, *Introduction to Textiles*, 3rd ed. (New York: John Wiley and Sons, 1970), pp. 317–318.

—*warp set* (Unit inferred from "Weaving is a method of producing cloth by interlacing two or more sets of yarns, at least one warp and one filling set . . . ." *Set* applies to both *warp* and *filling*, and is short for *set of yarn*. *Warp set* is in opposition to *filling set*.)

—*filling set* (*Filling* is an essential determinant as it indicates the function of the yarn and distinguishes it from the *warp*. Here again, *set* is short for *set of yarn*.)

—*warp; ends* (*Warp* is short for *warp yarn* below. *Ends* is given as a synonym of *warp*. *Warp* and *ends* are marked as terms by italics.)

—*filling; picks; weft* (*Filling* is short for *filling yarn* below. *Picks* and *weft* are given as synonyms of *filling*. Here too, *filling*, *picks* and *weft* are marked as terms by italics.)

—*woven fabric* (*Woven* is an essential determinant, specifying the type of fabric, as opposed to knitted, bonded or felt, for example, and the means by which it is produced.)

—*warp yarn* (Long form of *warp* above. *Extra* in *extra warp yarn* is inessential as it does not significantly modify the meaning of *warp yarn*.)

—*selvage* (Basic concept in the production of woven fabric; marked as a term by italics.)

—*filling yarn* (Long form of *filling* above.)

—*loom* (Basic concept in the production of woven fabric; marked as a term by italics.)

—*warp beam* (Partitive relationship to *loom*, opposed to *cloth beam*; marked as a term by italics.)

—*cloth beam* (Partitive relationship to *loom*, opposed to *warp beam*; marked as a term by italics.)

—*harness frame* (Partitive relationship to *loom*; marked as a term by italics.)

—*to form the weaving shed* (Would be entered on the terminology record as *to form a weaving shed*. Co-occurring expression; basic concept in the production of woven fabric.)

—*weaving shed* (*Weaving* is an essential determinant as it specifies a vital aspect of *shed*.)

—*heddle* (Partitive relationship to *loom*; marked as a term by italics.)

—*reed* (Partitive relationship to *loom*; marked as a term by italics.)

—*shuttle*; *bobbin* (Partitive relationship to *loom*; *bobbin* is given as a synonym of *shuttle*. Both are marked as terms by italics.)

—*eye of the heddle* (Would be entered on the terminology record as *eye of a heddle*. Less lexicalized expression similar to *eye of a needle*; *correct* in *eye of the correct heddle* is inessential.)

—*pattern* (Basic concept in the production of woven fabric.)

—*threading* (Basic concept in weaving preparation.)

—*cloth beam apron* (Partitive relationship to *cloth beam*.)

—*to form a shed* (Short for *to form a weaving shed* above.)

—*shed* (Short for *weaving shed* above; marked as a term by italics.)

—*harness* (Short for *harness frame* above.)

—*frame* (Short for *harness frame* above.)

—*tied-in knot* (*Tied-in* is an essential determinant as it indicates the type of knot.)

—*cloth apron* (Short for *cloth beam apron* above.)

## 8.1.1  Observations

A short text like this provides information that is important, but nonetheless incomplete. The terminologist would need to consult other sources for a fuller understanding of textiles in general and weaving in particular.

The most striking characteristic of the terminology identified is the abundance of synonyms. The text contains a number of undifferentiated synonyms, such as *warp* and *ends*, and *filling, picks* and *weft*. Other texts would need to be consulted to determine any differences in meaning or usage, and establish why some are given in the singular and others in the plural. Many of the terms detected have short forms or variants:[2] for example, *warp* and *warp yarn; filling* and *filling yarn; harness frame, harness* and *frame; cloth beam apron* and *cloth apron; weaving shed* and *shed*. These variants are important to note as they indicate the term forms used in context.

## 8.2  Selection of Contexts

When selecting a context, the terminologist attempts to cull as much relevant data as possible on the meaning of a term. Contexts are therefore selected according to the quality of the information they contain. The contexts appearing in this text can be selected and analyzed as follows:

*weaving*
> Weaving is a method (nature) of producing cloth (purpose) by interlacing (means) two or more sets of yarns (material) . . . at right angles to each other (means).[3] (Defining)

*produce cloth (to)*
> Weaving (means) is a method of producing cloth by interlacing (means) two or more sets of yarns (material) . . . at right angles to each other (means). (Explanatory)

*interlace sets of yarn (to)*
> Weaving is a method of producing cloth (purpose) by interlacing two or more sets of yarns, at least one warp and one filling set (material), at right angles to each other (position). (Explanatory)

---

2. See Chapter 12, *SYNONYMY*, section 12.1 for an explanation of variants.

3. The ellipsis indicates that information has been omitted.

*set of yarn*

> Weaving is a method of producing cloth by interlacing two or more sets of yarns . . . at right angles to each other. (Associative)

*yarn*

> Weaving is a method of producing cloth by interlacing two or more sets of yarns . . . . (Associative)

*filling set*

> Weaving is a method of producing cloth by interlacing two or more sets of yarns (nature), at least one warp and one filling set, at right angles to each other (position). (Explanatory)

*warp; ends; warp yarn*

> Weaving is a method of producing cloth by interlacing two or more sets of yarns (nature), at least one warp and one filling set . . . . The *warp* is also called *ends* . . . . The warp runs from front to back of the loom and lengthwise in a woven fabric (position). . . .
>
> In preparation for weaving, the warp yarns are . . . wound evenly on the warp beam (position) . . . . (Explanatory)

*selvage*

> Extra warp yarns (material) at each side [of the fabric] (location) form a *selvage* during weaving. (Explanatory)

*filling; picks; weft; filling yarn*

> Weaving is a method of producing cloth by interlacing two or more sets of yarns (nature), at least one warp and one filling set . . . . The *filling* is also called *picks*, or *weft*. . . . Filling yarns run across from side to side, or from selvage to selvage (position). (Explanatory)

*woven fabric*
> The warp runs from front to back of the loom and lengthwise in a woven fabric. (Associative)

*loom*
> The machine (nature) for weaving (purpose) is a *loom* . . . .
>
> Essential parts of the loom include the *warp beam*, . . . the *cloth beam*, . . . *harness frames*, . . . *heddles*, . . . the *reed*, . . . and *shuttles* or *bobbins* (components) . . . . (Defining)

*warp beam*
> Essential parts of the loom (nature) include the *warp beam*, on which the warp yarns are wound (purpose) . . . . (Explanatory)

*cloth beam*
> Essential parts of the loom (nature) include . . . the *cloth beam*, on which the cloth is wound as it is woven (purpose) . . . . (Explanatory)

*harness frame; harness; frame*
> Essential parts of the loom (nature) include . . . *harness frames* which carry the heddles (function), and which move up or down to form the weaving shed (function) . . . .
>
> During weaving, the harnesses are raised and lowered . . . causing a separation of the warp yarns as the heddles are carried up or down with the frames . . . . (Explanatory)

*form a weaving shed (to)*
> Essential parts of the loom include . . . *harness frames* which carry the heddles, and which move up or down to form the weaving shed . . . . (Associative)

*heddles*
> Essential parts of the loom (nature) include . . . *heddles*, each with an eye in the center (form), through which

the individual yarns are threaded (function), usually one yarn to a heddle.... (Explanatory)

*reed*

Essential parts of the loom (nature) include... the *reed*, which keeps the warp yarns separated (function), helps to determine cloth width (function), and acts as a beater (function).... (Explanatory)

*shuttle; bobbin*

Essential parts of the loom (nature) include... *shuttles* or *bobbins* for carrying the filling yarns across from side to side (function). (Explanatory)

*threading*

Each warp yarn... is drawn through the eye of the correct heddle (means) on the correct harness frame... and then is carried through the correct opening in the reed to the front of the loom (means) where all the warp yarns, when the threading is completed, are evenly tensioned.... (Explanatory)

*cloth beam apron; cloth apron*

Each warp yarn... is drawn through the eye of the correct heddle... and then is carried through the correct opening in the reed to the front of the loom (location) where all the warp yarns... are evenly tensioned and tied (function) to the cloth beam apron.... The shuttle carrying the filling yarn goes through the shed from one side to the other, and the yarn left by its passing is beaten forward by the reed against the tied-in knots at the cloth apron.... (Explanatory)

*eye of the heddle*

Each warp yarn... is drawn through the eye of the correct heddle.... (Associative)

*pattern*

During weaving, the harnesses are raised and lowered in an order determined by the pattern.... (Associative)

*weaving shed; shed*
>*Harness frames* ... move up or down to form the weaving shed . . . .
>
>Each warp yarn (material) must run straight from cloth beam to warp beam without being crossed with any other yarn; this is essential for raising and lowering the different harnesses (means of formation) to form a *shed*. (Explanatory)

*tied-in knots*
>All the warp yarns (material), when the threading is completed, are evenly tensioned and tied to the cloth beam apron. . . . The yarn left by its [the shuttle's] passing is beaten forward by the reed against the tied-in knots at the cloth apron (position) . . . . (Explanatory)

## 8.2.1 Observations

The majority of contexts are explanatory because the text itself is explanatory. The contexts selected contain as much pertinent information as possible, but even so they do not truly give a clear idea of what a loom looks like, how it operates, or how the weaving process is carried out. Since weaving equipment, materials and techniques are extremely concrete, illustrations would be useful in helping the terminologist fully grasp the concepts involved. Once again, this points up the need for supplementary sources of information.

# CHAPTER 9

# COMPARATIVE TERMINOLOGY

## 9.0 Introduction

The work methods outlined in the preceding chapters apply to monolingual as well as bilingual and multilingual research. In bilingual and multilingual research, however, the terminologist must go one step further and compare the source- and target-language terms—hence the name *comparative terminology*—in order to determine whether they are equivalent.

## 9.1 Full Equivalence

Two terms from different languages are considered to be fully equivalent when they have the same meaning and are used in the same way in a given subject field. *Ancienneté* in French and *seniority* in English, for example, are fully equivalent in that they represent the same concept in the field of human resources management—the privileged status achieved by an employee on the basis of length of service with an organization—and have the same usage, i.e. are both up to date, frequently and widely used, and belong to the same register.

Source- and target-language terms can be fully equivalent even if they represent a concept from a different point of view. For example, the act of placing a ban on the airing of a live broadcast is referred to as *décrocher* in French and *to black out* in English. The French term emphasizes the disconnection of the signal, whereas the English, the effect of doing so. This difference in point of view by no means compromises the equivalence of the terms, since they designate the same concept and are used in the same way in broadcast programming. The same can be said of the French term *héritage* and its English equivalent, *follow-on audience,* which in broadcast research refer to those viewers who have been sufficiently interested in one program to view another in the following time slot. The French term is figurative, whereas the English is more literal. Nonetheless, they are fully equivalent.

## 9.2 Partial Equivalence

Different language communities formulate and name concepts according to their own particular experience of the world. As a result, source-language terms sometimes cover only part of the concept represented by their so-called target-language equivalents, or are used in a more restricted manner.

### 9.2.1 Discrepancies in Meaning

Any discrepancy in meaning between a source-language term and its target-language equivalent must be identified by means of semantic labels.[1]

The most frequently encountered semantic difference in terminological research occurs when a term in one language is generic and its equivalent specific. *Table basse*, for example, in the field of home furnishings encompasses *coffee table*, *end table* and *lamp table*. *Auditeur* in broadcasting refers to both television *viewer* and radio *listener*. *Outdoor advertising* in publicity covers both *affichage extérieur* and *affichage transports*.

Since living language is constantly evolving, a term in one language can undergo a shift in meaning or acquire a new meaning, while its equivalent in another language remains unchanged. Take, for example, the French term *courbe*, which is used in the field of statistics. The first meaning of *courbe* is the graphic representation of the distribution of a variable. By extension, the term has come to refer to the distribution itself. The English term *curve* has not undergone the same shift in meaning, and refers strictly to the graphic represen-

---

1. See Chapter 10, *TERMINOLOGY RECORDS*, section 10.4.3.2 for a complete list of semantic labels.

tation of a distribution. For the two English terms *curve* and *distribution*, there is only one French term, *courbe*. *Curve* and *courbe* are equivalent when designating the graphic representation of a distribution, as are *distribution* and *courbe* when designating the distribution itself.

### 9.2.2 Discrepancies in Usage

Even when two terms from different languages cover precisely the same concept, they may be used in different ways. They may, for example, differ in register, geographic area of application, age or frequency of use.

## 9.3 Usage Labels

Any discrepancy in usage between a source-language term and its target-language equivalent must be identified by means of usage labels. The labels generally used to mark discrepancies in usage are *sociolinguistic, geographic, temporal* and *frequency labels*.[2]

### 9.3.1 Sociolinguistic Labels

Special languages are developed from the basis of the general language; they are subsystems which overlap general language and are therefore dependent on it. Like general language, special languages have different registers, which can influence the choice of appropriate expression.

The registers of both the general and special languages are characterized primarily by vocabulary or terminology—written or spoken—and depend both on the topic being discussed and the relationship of the people discussing it. The registers of the general language can be categorized as follows: **vulgar** (obscene or taboo language which is used to shock or offend); **slang** (deliberately unorthodox, popular, novel-sounding language which is derived largely from the private lingo of isolated groups); **informal or colloquial** (familiar

2. See Chapter 10, *TERMINOLOGY RECORDS*, section 10.4.3.2 for a complete list of usage labels.

language, often codified and abbreviated, used within the family and generally among people who know one another fairly well); **formal** (the language of the arts, science, business, law, etc., used in relatively learned or official contexts among people who have a more formal relationship); and **literary** (the characteristic expression of prose and verse).

*Food*, for example, can be referred to as *grub* or *chow* in a slang register, *food* in an informal or a formal register, and *sustenance* in a literary. *Tiredness* can be called *fatigue* in a formal register and *lassitude* in a literary. *To work* can be designated as *to slog* in an informal or colloquial register and *to toil* in a literary.

The registers of special languages can be described as follows: **jargon** (informal terminology used by professionals or tradespeople in informal situations); **commercial** (the brand names or trademarks under which different products and services are marketed); **in-house or firm** (terminology typically used by a particular organization or corporation); **customary** (terminology commonly used by experts and non-experts in formal or informal situations); and **technical or scientific** (formal terminology used primarily by subject-field experts in relatively formal situations).

For example, job titles in television production such as *pancake turner*, *gaffer* and *juicer* are jargon and are synonyms of the more customary terms *turntable operator*, *lighting technician* and *electrician*. Commercial terms or trademarks such as *aspirin* and *gravol* are referred to as *acetylsalicylic acid tablet* and *anti-nauseant tablet* in a technical register. An in-house term like *rightsizing*, i.e. reducing a company's workforce as a result of dwindling resources, is called *downsizing* in a customary register.

A concept may be designated in one language by a number of terms from different registers and in another language by one term from one register. For example, the term *pancake turner* mentioned above, which refers to a studio technician in charge of operating the turntable, is also referred to as *spinner*, *record operator* and *turntable operator*. For these four English terms, two jargon (*pancake turner* and *spinner*) and two customary (*record operator* and *turntable operator*), there is one French equivalent: *opérateur-disques*. Such discrepancies in register must be duly identified on the terminology record to alert users about limitations in equivalence and inform them about the circumstances in which terms are appropriate.

### 9.3.2  Geographic Labels

Concepts are often represented by different terms in different parts of the world. For example, the French broadcasting term *audience* is used primarily in France and *its synonym*, *auditoire*, primarily in Québec. In botany, the plant that answers to the name of *devil's ivy* in Britain is called *pothos* in the United States, and *Scindapsus*, its Latin name, in both countries. Geographic labels are used to identify any strictly regional uses.

### 9.3.3  Temporal Labels

When a term has disappeared from current use but is retained for historical purposes, it is labelled **obsolete**, such as *purchase* in the sense of pillage. **Archaic** is applied to terms that are no longer in regular use but may be found occasionally in certain contexts, such as *chain* in the sense of broadcast network. **Neologism** is used to identify terms that have recently entered a special language, such as *ubiquity* in the sense of technological openness of universal information networks.

### 9.3.4  Frequency Labels

The terms researched and recorded in terminology are considered to be frequently used unless they are labelled otherwise. A term that is used infrequently is labelled **rare**. For example, in statistical surveys, the individual who fills out the survey questionnaire is usually called the *respondent*, but in rare instances is referred to as the *informant*.

## 9.4 Limitations of Partial Equivalence

When two terms from different languages are only partially equivalent, the possibility of using one term in exactly the same meaning and situation as the other is limited. *Coffee table* can be rendered by *table basse* only if the user does not have to identify a specific type of table. *Auditeur* can be referred to as *listener* only in the context of radio. *Opérateur-disques* can be called *pancake turner* only in a television studio among technicians in the know.

It might seem simpler to dismiss the whole question of partial equivalence, with all its complexities and nuances, and focus strictly on full equivalence. However, it is not always possible to establish full equivalence; moreover it is essential to acknowledge the right of a language community to express itself in the terms that are natural to it.

## 9.5 Textual Match: The Key to Determining Equivalence of Concepts

*Textual match* refers to the correspondence of semantic features appearing in the source- and target-language contexts cited on a bilingual terminology record. A textual match serves to confirm that the source- and target-language terms represent the same concept and are therefore equivalent.

Consider the following bilingual record:

---

tête de ligne    COLTE    80    325

Centre de contrôle d'où les signaux, captés au moyen d'antennes ou reçus par micro-ondes, sont distribués par câbles coaxiaux.

headend    FOBRO    78    459

The location from which the TV signals received directly off the air and the imported signals received by microwave are sent to homes by cable.

---

The French and English contexts can be analyzed as follows:

Nature: **centre de contrôle**
Function: d'où les **signaux, captés au moyen d'antennes ou reçus par micro-ondes**
Function: d'où les signaux . . . sont **distribués par câbles coaxiaux**

Nature: **location**
Function: from which the **TV signals received directly off the air** and the **imported signals received by microwave**
Function: from which the **TV signals** . . . **are sent to homes by cable**

The semantic features in the French and English contexts match or correspond to a large extent; this enables the terminologist to determine that the terms cover the same concept and are, in fact, equivalent. In theory, a solid textual match is essential for determining equivalence. In practice, contexts with an explicit textual match cannot always be found; in such cases, equivalence can be determined through the implicit meaning provided by the contexts. Only specialists or terminologists familiar with the field can judge the validity of a record without an explicit textual match.

It may be tempting to think that the apparent correspondence of two terms from different languages can take the place of a textual match. However, this is absolutely untrue and a trap to be avoided. As we have seen, *publicité extérieure* is not equivalent to *outdoor advertising*. Careful analysis of their contexts indicates that *affichage extérieur* is equivalent to *outdoor advertising* and *publicité extérieure* to *out-of-home advertising*.

A textual match can also consist of corresponding illustrations, drawings or photographs. Illustrations are particularly useful in establishing equivalence in the case of hardware, equipment made up of various parts, or complex technology.

## 9.6 Conclusion

In bilingual and multilingual research, determining the equivalence of terms involves identifying the concept they represent and analyzing the context—sociolinguistic, temporal and geographic—in which they are used.

Analysis of the source- and target-language terms necessarily includes an investigation and a comparison of their respective semantic features. Any discrepancies in meaning or usage must be identified by means of semantic or usage labels.

# EXERCISES

1. Research the meaning and usage of the following pairs of terms, and identify any discrepancies by means of semantic or usage labels.

   Field: Audiovisual
   *baladeur*
   *walkman*

   Field: Information systems
   *informatique*
   *data processing*

   Field: Industrial relations
   *travail au noir*
   *secondary employment*

   Field: Broadcasting
   *substitution de signal*
   *cherrypicking*

   *travail au noir*
   *moonlighting*

   *câblodistribution*
   *cable television*

2. Find definitions or defining contexts for the following pairs of terms. Analyze the semantic features provided by these contexts and establish a textual match.

   Field: Broadcasting
   *console de bruitage*
   *cocktail bar*

   Field: Stationery
   *papier autocopiant*
   *carbonless paper*

   Field: Sports
   *athlétisme*
   *track and field*

# CHAPTER 10

# TERMINOLOGY RECORDS

## 10.0 Introduction

The practical approach taken to terminological research in this handbook points up the need for terminologists to work with living language. Vocabularies, glossaries and specialized dictionaries do not give terminologists the flexibility they need for recording the results of their research and maintaining terminological data. Once these works are published, the information they contain is fixed and difficult to modify.[1] A terminology record, however, is easy to file, change, update or replace, and thus constitutes an ideal medium for recording up-to-the-minute terminological data.

## 10.1 Definition of Terminology Record

A terminology record is a paper or electronic document which contains readily accessible information on a term specific to a subject field, on the concept it represents, and on the source in which it is found.

## 10.2 Format

In computerized terminology files, the format depends on the management system. Some systems use a sequential format in which each field on the record appears successively in a predetermined order. Other systems use a condensed format enabling the user to view the entire record at a glance. Both formats offer a number of advantages.

For manual terminology records, however, the condensed format is definitely preferable. With this format, records are

---

1. While much progress has been made in recent years in computerizing such works, the updating process remains relatively long and unwieldy.

easier to consult, file and store, although there are certain constraints:[2] contexts have to be truncated and codes have to be used to represent the various parameters.[3] As a result, the condensed format encourages the terminologist to be extremely selective in the choice of information, since there is no room for superfluous data on the record.

## 10.3 Content

Monolingual terminology records are divided into 10 fields, which are reserved for the information outlined below.

**Field 1—Entry:** Field 1 is reserved for the entry term, which must appear in its usual lexical form, i.e. the first letter must not be capitalized unless the entry is a proper noun. Nouns must be entered in the singular, unless the plural has special reference (see *Field 5—Grammatical Labels* below for an explanation), and verbs must be entered in the infinitive. The entry must appear in its usual order, i.e. it must not be inverted, except the infinitive marker of English verbs. For example, *to fine tune* would be entered as *fine tune (to)*.

If the source cited provides any synonyms or variants, they must be entered in this field after the entry term. The entry and its synonyms or variants must be separated by a semicolon.

In computerized files, each synonym or variant must also be declared an entry so they can be used to access the record.

---

2. The sequential format, which is being used more and more in computerized terminology files, has constraints as well, but fewer than the condensed format. While many of the parameters on sequential format records must also be represented by codes, the definitions and contexts do not have to be truncated to the same extent.

3. Any of the data elements entered on a terminology record to qualify the usage or status of a term are referred to as parameters. These parameters may be either terminological (usage labels, grammatical labels) or technical (*standardized*). (*Vocabulary of Terminology*. Ottawa: Terminology Directorate, Secretary of State, 1983.)

In manual files, each synonym or variant must be entered on a separate record which is cross-referenced to the main record.

**Field 2—Source**: Bibliographic reference for the text cited on the record to document the entry. The source is entered in the form of a code. A separate record, which provides the bibliographic reference in full, must be prepared for the source code. (Examples of source code records are provided in 10.4.3.1.)

**Field 3—Date of Publication**: Year in which the source was published. Usually only the last two digits are indicated.

**Field 4—Volume, Issue and Page Numbers**: Volume number if the source comprises more than one volume, issue number if the source is a periodical, and the page on which the information cited is found.

**Field 5—Grammatical Labels**: This field is reserved for labels of terminological import. The **part of speech** is labelled only when it could be ambiguous. For example, *cross over*, an audience measurement term, could be a noun, adjective or verb, thus the part of speech would need to be marked. The **number** is indicated only when a term must be entered in the plural to cover the concept recorded. For example, *ratings*, another audience measurement term, would need to be entered in the plural and marked as such since it represents the following: "calculations of the [audience's] acceptance of a programming channel or individual show."[4] The **gender** in languages other than English is indicated only when it might be unclear; for example, the gender of certain neologisms in French (such as *différé*, the equivalent of *delayed broadcast*) or of some terms French has borrowed from another language (such as *interview*) would need to be labelled.

---

4. Don Schiller, *CATV Program Origination and Production* (Pennsylvania: Tab Books, 1979), p. 246.

**Field 6—Usage and Semantic Labels**: Reserved for duly documented characteristics, such as differences in geographic or temporal usage, in register, or in meaning between the entry term and its synonyms. The codes for all such labels are provided in 10.4.3.2.

**Field 7—Context**: Excerpt from the source documenting the entry term, or definition if the source is a lexicographic or encyclopedic work.

**Field 8—Fields**: For records prepared as part of subject-field research, the lower three levels of the subject-field breakdown (see Chapter 6, section 6.1.5, *Preparing a Breakdown of the Subject Field*); for records prepared as part of term research, the general field of application and the specific subfield. The terminology record is valid only for the field and subfield(s) indicated.

**Field 9—Author and Date**: Identification of the person who prepared the record and the date on which it was prepared.

**Field 10—Access Keys**: Terms or term elements that can be used to access a record if the entry is unknown. Access keys can include any known components of the entry, terms related to the entry, semantic features appearing in the context cited, and the subfields in which the entry is used. In computerized files, each of these terms must be declared an access key. In manual files, each must appear on a separate record which is cross-referenced to the main record.

### Example of a Monolingual Record

Field 1:    warp; ends
Field 2:    STOTE
Field 3:    70
Field 4:    317
Field 5:
Field 6:

Field 7: The *warp* is also called *ends* . . . . The warp runs from front to back of the loom and lenghtwise in a woven fabric.

Field 8: textiles; weaving

Field 9: RD (Robert Dubuc) 88-11-07

Field 10: loom; woven fabric

**Secondary Records**

1. Record of source code:

   STOTE
   Stout, Evelyn E. *Introduction to Textiles.* New York: John Wiley and Sons, 1970.

2. Record of synonym cross-referenced to main record:

   ends
   See warp

3. Records of access key cross-referenced to main record:

   loom
   Also see warp

   woven fabric
   Also see warp

It should be noted that the cross-reference marker on records of synonyms is *See* in English and *Voir* in French, whereas that on records of access keys is *Also see* and *Voir aussi*.

**Example of a Bilingual Record**

The first seven fields on a bilingual record are the same as those on a monolingual record. The second seven fields—fields 8 to 14—are a repeat of fields 1 to 7, but are reserved for the target-language information. The field and subfield(s), author and date are entered in fields 15 and 16 on a bilingual record. Access keys, entered in field 10 of a monolingual record, are not needed on a bilingual record because a bilingual record contains the source-language term, which is used to access the record.

Field 1:   chaîne; fil de chaîne
Field 2:   MEUTE
Field 3:   88
Field 4:   117
Field 5:
Field 6:
Field 7:   La chaîne, ou si l'on veut le fil de chaîne, s'étend d'une extrémité à l'autre du métier à tisser, de l'ensouple au rouleau toilier. Elle est disposée dans le sens de la longueur d'un tissu.
Field 8:   warp; ends
Field 9:   STOTE
Field 10:  70
Field 11:  317
Field 12:
Field 13:
Field 14:  The *warp* is also called *ends* . . . . The warp runs from front to back of the loom and lengthwise in a woven fabric.
Field 15:  textile; tissage
Field 16:  RD (Robert Dubuc)  88-11-07

No matter which format is used, sequential or condensed, a bilingual record should contain these 16 fields. To create a trilingual record, seven fields (fields 15 to 21) would be added for the third-language information, and fields 15 and 16—for the field and subfield(s), author and date—would become fields 22 and 23.

**Secondary Records**

1.  Records of source codes:

    MEUTE
    Meunier, Jean. *Initiation aux textiles*. Paris: Edidon, 1988.

STOTE
Stout, Evelyn E. *Introduction to Textiles*. New York: John Wiley and Sons, 1970.

2. Records of synonyms:

fils de chaîne
Voir chaîne

ends
See warp

## 10.4 Processing Terminology Records

### 10.4.1 Cases of Synonymy

Only synonyms documented by the source cited on a record can be included in field 1 with the entry term. If synonyms are derived from other sources, they must be entered on separate records which are cross-referenced to the main record. In bilingual terminology, both the source-language entry and the target-language equivalent may have synonyms.

Let's assume that French is the source language and English the target language. Source A contains the term *marque maison* with sufficient information to elucidate its meaning, i.e. a label under which a distributor sells products manufactured by someone else. Source B documents the term *marque de distributeur* and offers a sufficiently similar context to establish that *marque maison* and *marque de distributeur* are synonyms. A record should be prepared for the first term, *marque maison,* citing source A. "Voir marque de distributeur" should be indicated at the end of field 7, which contains the explanatory or defining context. A record should then be prepared for the synonym *marque de distributeur,* citing source B and providing a cross-reference to *marque maison* at the end of field 7.

The target-language equivalent also has a synonym. Source C documents the term *private brand* and provides a context rich in information. Source D documents the term *distributor's brand* and provides a sufficiently similar context to establish that *private brand* and *distributor's brand* are synonyms. A record should be prepared for the first term, *private brand*, citing source C. "See distributor's brand" should be indicated at the end of field 7. A second record should then be prepared for the synonym *distributor's brand*, citing source D and providing a cross-reference to *private brand* at the end of field 7.

**Examples**

RECORD 1

marque maison                A
(Context) Voir marque de distributeur

private brand                C
(context)

RECORD 2

marque maison  (with no other indications)
distributor's brand          D
(context)

RECORD 3

marque de distributeur       B
(context) Voir marque maison

private brand (with no other indications)

RECORD 4

marque de distributeur (with no other indications)

distributor's brand (with no other indications)

Record 1 is the main record. The context cited on record 1 does not have to be repeated on record 2. Similarly, the English contexts for *private brand* and *distributor's brand* appear on records 1 and 2, so they do not have to be reproduced on records 3 and 4. Reference to *marque maison* on record 3 enables the user to retrieve all the information needed, since records 1 and 2 will be consecutive in both a manual and computerized terminology file, as will records 3 and 4.

Processing records with a single source documenting synonyms is much simpler. Let's take the example of *chaîne* and *warp* provided above.

RECORD 1

chaîne; fil de chaîne      (source)
(context documenting synonymy)

warp; ends      (source)
(context documenting synonymy)

RECORD 2

fil de chaîne (without any other indications)
Voir chaîne

In a manual file, the source-language term is consulted, i.e. either *chaîne*, which provides the French synonym as well as the target-language equivalent and its synonym, or *fil de chaîne*, which refers the user to the main record under *chaîne* for all the necessary information on *fil de chaîne*.

In a computerized file, the entry terms and synonyms are all declared entries, so the second record is unnecessary.

### 10.4.2 Contexts

Contexts often contain information that is superfluous, i.e. that is inessential for an adequate understanding of the term. To avoid reproducing contexts that are needlessly long, superfluous information can be deleted, provided the deletion is clearly marked by an ellipsis. For example, the third paragraph of the text on weaving in Chapter 8 discusses the essential parts of a loom. Each part constitutes a terminology unit, but it would be unnecessarily cumbersome to reproduce the entire paragraph for every part. The inessential information can simply be deleted. For example, the context for *heddle* could be shortened to: "Essential parts of the loom include . . . *heddles*, each with an eye in the center, through which the individual yarns are threaded, usually one yarn to a heddle . . . ." The ellipsis indicates that information has been omitted.

When shortening a context, it is sometimes necessary to add information to ensure that the context reads properly. Any information added should appear in square brackets. Consider the following text, which explains the meanings of the term *chaîne*:

> La chaîne, ou si l'on veut le fil de chaîne, est montée de l'avant à l'arrière du métier à tisser. Fixée d'abord sur l'ensouple, elle est nouée à la bande-amorce du rouleau toilier. Elle peut désigner soit un fil de chaîne pris isolément, soit l'ensemble des fils de chaîne. La chaîne se divise en deux nappes pour former la foule. C'est dans la foule que passe la duite, c'est-à-dire le fil de trame contenu dans la bobine et laissé dans la foule. Dans le tissu constitué, elle forme l'ensemble des fils parallèles dans le sens de la longueur.[5]

This context can be shortened as follows, yet still document both meanings of *chaîne*: "La chaîne . . . peut désigner soit un fil de chaîne pris isolément, soit l'ensemble des fils de chaîne . . . [qui] dans le tissu constitué . . . forme . . . [les] fils parallèles dans le sens de la longueur." Note that the deletions are marked by an ellipsis and the additions are indicated in square brackets.

### 10.4.3 Codes

In order to save time and space, codes are used to represent some of the information appearing on terminology records. The codes used, however, must be immediately recognizable so that the terminology record remains practical.

---

5. Jean Meunier, *Initiation aux textiles* (Paris: Edidon, 1988), p. 117.

### 10.4.3.1 Sources

The sources of terminological information cannot be given in full on terminology records because of space limitations on manual records and memory limitations in computerized files.

The method of creating source codes which is generally used in terminology consists in combining letters of the author's name and title of the work to form an acronym. Source codes usually include five letters, which are combined as follows:

(a) If the main word in the title begins with a vowel, the author's surname is cut after the second consonant, then the initial letters of the main word in the title are added to form a five-letter acronym. The code always begins with the initial letters of the author's surname.

For example, the source code for *Lives of the Artist* (AR) by George Vasture (VAS) would be VASAR.

(b) If the main word in the title begins with a consonant, the author's surname is cut after the first vowel, then the initial letters of the main word in the title are added.

For example, the code for *Understanding Broadcasting* (BRO) by Aegean S. Foster (FO) would be FOBRO.

(c) In the case of a journal or review whose title consists of one word, up to the first five letters of the word are selected. If the title consists of two or more words, the two main words are cut and joined according to the guidelines above so as to form a five-letter acronym.

For example: *Meta*—Complete title would be selected and capitalized.

*National Geographic*—NAGEO

Words in a title which identify the type of document, i.e. dictionary, vocabulary, glossary, handbook, guide, review, journal, etc., should not be used in the code, as they do not give an idea of the subject.

A source code record must be prepared for each source code. Source code records for books must provide the author's surname, and first name or initial. If there are two authors, the surname and first name of the second are not inverted; if there are more than two authors, "et al" is indicated after the first. The title of the work is italicized, and is followed by the name of the editor, compiler or translator and edition or volume, if applicable, as well as the place of publication, the name of the publisher, and the publication date. In the case of a collective work, the compiler or editor's name is provided instead of an author's, and is followed by "comp." or "ed.", as the case may be.

Source code records for journals or reviews provide the title, either underlined or italicized, followed by the volume number, issue number and date. Source code records for conference proceedings provide the conference title, again italicized, followed by the place of publication, the name of the publisher and the publication date.

**Examples of Source Code Records**

KESTA
Kendall, Maurice, and William Buckland. *A Dictionary of Statistical Terms*. Edinburgh: Oliver and Boyd, 1971.

EBROA
Eastman, Susan Tyler et al. *Broadcast Programming: Strategies for Winning Television and Radio Audiences*. U.S.A.: Wadsworth Inc., 1981.

MCIMI
McIntyre, Joan, comp. *Mind in the Waters*. Toronto: McClelland and Stewart, 1974.

TRACO
*Proceedings of the First North American Translators Congress*. U.S.A.: Learned Information Inc., 1986.

### 10.4.3.2 Labels

The large number of usage, semantic and grammatical labels can certainly pose a problem, since they all need to be identified by a meaningful symbol. While there are no firmly established symbols for the labels that may be used on terminology records, the following abbreviations are relatively widely used.

(a) **Geographic labels**: CA (Canada), US (United States), GB (Great Britain) for English, and CF (Canadian French), FF (French of France), BF (Belgian French), SF (Swiss French) and AF (African French) for French.

Geographic labels are used to identify parallel usage, in different countries or geographical regions, of terms that represent the same concept in the same subject field.

(b) **Semantic labels**: GEN (generic), SP (specific), CAU (cause), EF (effect), PAR (part), WH (whole), CON (concrete), AB (abstract), MEL (meliorative) and PEJ (pejorative).

(c) **Sociolinguistic labels**: JAR (jargon), TECH (technical), SC (scientific) and R (registered trademark).

(d) **Temporal labels**: ARCH (archaic), OUTM (outmoded), NEOL (neologism).

(e) **Frequency labels**: COM (commonly used), RARE (rare).

It is important to bear in mind that semantic, sociolinguistic, temporal and frequency labels are to be used only to mark discrepancies in meaning or usage between a term and its synonym in the same language, or between a term in one language and its equivalent in another.

(f) **Grammatical labels**: N (noun), ADJ (adjective), V (verb), TV (transitive verb), IV (intransitive verb), M (masculine), F (feminine), S (singular), PL (plural).

Grammatical labels are to be used only if they have terminological import (see 10.3 *Field 5—Grammatical Labels* for an explanation).

### 10.4.3.3 Fields

The field and subfields on terminology records may be indicated in full or shortened. If shortened, it is important to ensure that the abbreviation selected is original and not being used for another purpose.

### 10.4.3.4 Author and Date

When records are included in a central file with numerous contributors, the author of the record must be identified by an exclusive code. All author codes must be explained in the contributor code file. The date on which the record was prepared must accompany the author's identification, and should be indicated in accordance with ISO recommendations, i.e. year, month, day.

## 10.5 Conclusion

In preparing a terminology record, it is important to keep in mind that the information recorded is constantly changing. A terminology record is not a permanent document carved in stone, but rather a working document that attests to usage at a given time and in a given place. It is essential that the record, while remaining simple, be prepared according to well-established standards so that the information provided can be properly validated.

# APPENDIX

Example of a bilingual record in condensed format:

| 1 | 2 | 3 | 4 | 5 | 6 |
|---|---|---|---|---|---|
| chaîne; fil de chaîne | MEUTE | 88 | 117 | | |

| 7 |
|---|
| La chaîne, ou si l'on veut le fil de chaîne, s'étend d'une extrémité à l'autre du métier à tisser, de l'ensouple au rouleau toilier. Elle est disposée dans le sens de la longueur d'un tissu. |

| 8 | 9 | 10 | 11 | 12 | 13 |
|---|---|---|---|---|---|
| warp; ends | STOTE | 70 | 317 | | |

| 14 |
|---|
| The *warp* is also called *ends* . . . . The warp runs from front to back of the loom and lengthwise in a woven fabric. |

| 15 | 16 |
|---|---|
| weaving; textiles | RD 88-11-07 |

The numbers correspond to the fields discussed in 10.3 above.

# EXERCISES

1. Find a French text on weaving that covers the same subject as Evelyn Stout's text provided in Chapter 8. Analyze the terms and concepts in these two texts, and prepare bilingual records for them.

2. Prepare 10 bilingual records on the subject of your choice, in accordance with the guidelines provided in this and the preceding chapters.

# CHAPTER 11

# DEFINITIONS IN TERMINOLOGY

## 11.0 Introduction

The purpose of a definition in terminology is to provide a clear understanding of the meaning of a term specific to a given subject field. To achieve this, a definition need only provide the essential characteristics of a term as it is used in a particular field or subfield. In this respect, terminological definitions differ from lexicographic and encyclopedic definitions, which list all the meanings of a word in all its areas of application, and present the defined meanings in an orderly fashion according to logical or historical criteria.

Terminological definitions are used primarily in vocabularies. Term banks may start using definitions formulated from information obtained from oral and written sources, because the *Copyright Act* prohibits reproduction of quoted material on a medium accessible by the public.

## 11.1 Rules of Definition

Traditional rules, derived from Aristotle's *Topics*,[1] have been laid down for evaluating definitions. Four such rules apply to definitions in terminology.

### 11.1.1 A definition must not be expressed in obscure language.

The following definition of *cordierite*: "An orthorhombic mineral, bluish in colour and of composition $Al_3(Mg, Fe^{2+})_2Si_5Al0_{18}$", may seem obscure to the layman, but is intelligible to the geologist, for whom it is intended. So it is not obscure, but justifiably technical.

---

1. R. Robinson, *Definition*, p. 140.

However, Herbert Spencer's definition of *evolution* as "an integration of matter and concomitant dissipation of motion, during which the matter passes from an indefinite, incoherent homogeneity to a definite, coherent heterogeneity, and during which the retained motion undergoes a parallel transformation"[2] is obscure, because it attempts to explain the unknown with the even more unknown, and thus fails in its purpose.

### 11.1.2 A definition must be neither too broad nor too narrow.

The following definition of *talent*: "The ability to compose beautiful lyrics while taking a bath," is too narrow, because it excludes many cases to which *talent* may legitimately be applied. If broadened to "the ability to do something," the term's range of application extends to anyone able to perform anything in any way whatsoever. The definition is now clearly too broad.

Thus, a definition should neither include things to which a term does not apply, nor omit essential things to which it does apply. According to a traditional rule of logic, it should be equivalent to the term being defined, that is, able to replace it in any statement without altering the meaning of that statement.

### 11.1.3 A definition must not be circular.

The standard rule asserts that a definition should not use the term being defined or any grammatical variation of it. For example, "one who studies or specializes in herpetology" would constitute a circular definition of *herpetologist*. However, the standard version of the circularity rule is not always strictly observed in terminology, since it is acceptable in certain cases to define a term by means of one of its grammatical variations, provided the grammatical variation

---

2. I.M. Copi, *Introduction to Logic*, p. 157.

is also defined. Thus, the above definition of *herpetologist* would be acceptable as long as a noncircular definition of *herpetology* were provided separately.

### 11.1.4 A definition must not be negative where it can be affirmative.

According to this rule, a definition should explain what a term means, not what it does not mean. To define *chair* as "not a bed and not a couch" is to fail to explain its meaning. Nevertheless, there are many terms which are essentially negative in meaning and which require negative definitions. For example, *undifferentiated* means "having no special structure or function". *Achromatic* means "having no colour". A negative definition of a negative term can be effective since its point of reference is an implied alternative.[3]

## 11.2 Methods of Definition

There are several methods of definition used in terminology. The choice of method depends on the nature of the concept to be defined, the purpose of the definition, the information available, and the requirements of the user.

### 11.2.1 Definition by Genus and Difference

This method consists in naming the larger class or **genus** to which a concept belongs, then specifying a characteristic that differentiates it from everything else in that class. The ancient definition of *man* as "a rational animal" is an example of **definition by genus and difference**; *man* falls within the larger class of "animal", and is distinguished from the rest of that class by "rationality".[4]

**Definition by genus and difference** is the oldest and best-known method. It is widely used in both lexicography and

---

3. *Ibid.*, p. 157.
4. Robinson, p. 96.

terminology to define concepts that have complex properties, i.e. that can be analyzed according to class and specific difference.[5]

### 11.2.2 Partition Definition

A **partition definition** is a method of specifying a whole by its parts, and can be given in addition to a **definition by genus and difference** when referring to an object consisting of several parts. For example, *evening dress* can be defined partitively as "men's clothing consisting of a tailcoat and matching trousers (usually in black or midnight blue), a white stiff-bosomed shirt and a white bow tie". "Men's clothing" is the whole; "tailcoat", "black or midnight blue matching trousers", "white stiff-bosomed shirt" and "white bow tie" are the various parts.[6]

### 11.2.3 Definition by Description

This method describes a concept by listing its essential characteristics. The nature, material, purpose, means, cause and effect are among the most important characteristics, whereas time and place are considered nonessential. For example, *mirror* can be defined as "a polished surface, usually made of glass, that forms images by reflection". Its **nature** is described as "a polished surface", the **material** it is made of is "glass", its **purpose is** "to form images", and the **means** by which it does so is "by reflection".

The descriptive method has become solidly entrenched in terminological work as it encompasses answers to the questions most often asked by the terminologist researching the concept covered by a term: What is it? Where does it come from? What does it look like? What is it made of? What is it used for? and so on.

---

5. Copi, p. 154.

6. I. Dahlbert, "Terminological Definitions: Characteristics and Demands," p. 23.

### 11.2.4 Operational Definition

An **operational definition** consists in describing the performance of observable and repeatable operations. For example, *product* can be defined as "the number resulting from the multiplication together of two or more numbers".[7]

Some social scientists have incorporated this relatively new technique into their own disciplines, attempting to replace abstract definitions of *mind*, for example, by operational definitions referring exclusively to physiology and behaviour.[8] Terminologists have likewise adopted this method to define a wide range of processes, methods, mechanisms, and machines by describing how they are conducted or the manner in which they operate or function.

### 11.2.5 Synonymous Definition

The synonymous method consists in giving users a term with the same meaning as the term being defined, but with which they are already familiar. For example, *bellis perennis* can be defined by its synonym *daisy*.

This method is commonly used in dictionaries; however, its applicability in terminology is somewhat limited. This is partly because of the nature of synonyms in special languages and partly because most users require more information than such a definition can provide.[9] Although of limited value on its own, a synonymous definition can prove useful when combined with other methods.

## 11.3 Construction of Definitions

### 11.3.1 Choice of Method

Before a definition can be formulated, a method of defining must be determined. The choice of method depends to some

---

7. Copi, p. 151.

8. *Ibid.*

9. M.J.C. Sager, "Definitions in Terminology," p. 122.

extent on the nature of the concept being defined. For example, for objects consisting of several parts, such as *evening dress*, a **partition definition** is the logical choice—an **operational definition** would be completely meaningless.

However, many concepts can be defined by a number of different methods. *Cake*, for instance, can be defined generically (by genus and difference) as a sweet bread, partitively by listing the ingredients, and operationally by describing the recipe for making it.[10] The choice of method, then, also depends on the purpose of the definition and the requirements of the user.

### 11.3.2  Choice of Defining Terms

No matter which method is chosen, a definition always begins with the same part of speech as the term being defined.

#### 11.3.2.1  Defining Nouns

A noun is defined by a noun or noun phrase. A definition of a countable noun, i.e. one that can form a plural, usually begins with the indefinite article "a", for example: "*techno-casualty*—**a** person who is unemployed because his or her function has been taken over by computers or other machinery". A definition of an uncountable noun usually begins with the definite article "the", for example: "*audiodontics*—**the** study of the relationship of teeth to hearing".

#### 11.3.2.2  Defining Verbs

A definition of a verb begins with a verb or verb phrase in the infinitive form, thus accompanied by "to", for example: "*airdash*—to rush by airplane"; "*auralize*—to hear mentally".

#### 11.3.2.3  Defining Adjectives

A definition of an adjective begins with:

---

10. Dahlbert, p. 28.

(a) an adjective, for example: "*congenial*—user-friendly";

(b) a participle which functions as an adjective, for example: "*ageist*—prejudiced or discriminating against older people as a group"; "*disinformative*—pretending to inform but actually giving incomplete or otherwise misleading information"; or

(c) a prepositional phrase which functions as an adjective, for example: "*proactive*—of or relating to a policy of anticipating trends and working to promote their development;" "*back-of-the-book*—of or relating to printed or broadcast material of general interest."

### 11.3.2.4 Defining Adverbs

A definition of an adverb begins with an adverb or a prepositional phrase which functions as an adverb. For example, *hyperacutely* may be defined as "excessively", and *utopianly* as "in a visionary or impractical way".

## 11.4 Good Defining Practices

### 11.4.1 Adequacy

A definition should be adequate; in other words, it should define what it sets out to define (and not overdefine it, underdefine it or define something else). This key point is hilariously illustrated by Sidney Landau in his handbook on dictionaries. Landau writes:

> The definition of *frog test* in *Butterworths Medical Dictionary* is my favorite medical definition. I quote it in full: *frog test*—a test used to indicate pregnancy, in which a frog is used.
>
> This definition has an engaging simplicity and directness that I find charming. But one does wonder how the frog is used. Do woman and frog stare at one another to see who blinks first? (If the woman, she's pregnant.) Is the

test positive if the woman's touch turns the frog into a prince?[11]

In this example, the definition is not too broad, it simply does not provide *adequate* information for a clear understanding of the term.

### 11.4.2 Brevity

A definition should be as concise as possible, and usually no longer than one sentence or phrase. Although some authors believe that a definition can almost always be truer by being longer, others feel a definition is made better by being shorter since it is less likely to be redundant, overly wordy or include nonessential information.

### 11.4.3 Clarity

A definition should be free of ambiguity of form or content. Take the following definition of *Clio*: "a gold statuette awarded annually to outstanding commercial work by judges of the American Television & Radio Commercials Festival." According to the wording and structure of this definition, the statuette is awarded to commercial work, and this work is done by the judges. Logic would dictate that it is awarded by the judges for outstanding commercial work.

## 11.5 Information for a Definition

The information for a definition is obtained from the oral and written sources located during research. The semantic features provided by these sources can be identified, analyzed, and used to formulate a definition. Take the following written source, for example:

> A first step in understanding tides of Cape Cod is to study the manner in which the water level rises and falls. A simple way to do this would be to make a *tide staff* and attach it to the side of a wharf in a well-protected harbor.... The tide staff is simply a long flat board which is

---

11. S.I. Landau, *Dictionaries: The Art and Craft of Lexicography*, p. 146.

marked off into units of feet, numbered from zero at the bottom to, say, fifteen feet at the top, like a large ruler.[12]

The semantic features provided by this context are as follows: to study the manner in which the water level rises and falls to understand the tides (purpose); a long flat board (nature); marked off into units of feet, numbered from zero at the bottom to fifteen feet at the top (nature, i.e. a measure).

### 11.5.1   Formulating a Definition

A definition of *tide staff* can be formulated on the basis of the information provided above. It is important, however, to bear in mind the rules and methods of definition, the guidelines for defining terms and the recommended defining practices described earlier in this chapter. The method of definition that would best describe *tide staff*, in light of the information at hand, is the descriptive method. Since *tide staff* is a noun, the defining term should also be a noun. A definition by description can be formulated as follows:

*Tide staff*—a long flat board, marked off into units of feet from zero at the bottom to fifteen at the top, used to study variations in the water level between high and low tide.

## 11.6   Conclusion

The purpose of a definition in terminology is to provide the user with a clear understanding of the meaning of a term in a specific subject field. There are no hard-and-fast rules as to how this can be achieved; different methods of definition can be combined, illustrations can be provided, and so on. However, if the guidelines presented in this chapter are followed, chances are that the results will be quite adequate.

---

12. Arthur N. Strahler, *A Geologist's View of Cape Cod* (Orleans, Massachusetts: Parnassus Imprints, 1996), p. 58.

# BIBLIOGRAPHY

Copi, Irving M. *Introduction to Logic*. New York: Macmillan Publishing Company, 1978.

Dahlbert, Ingetraut. "Terminological Definitions: Characteristics and Demands." In *Problèmes de la définition et de la synonymie en terminologie*. Québec: GIRSTERM, 1983.

International Organization for Standardization. International Standard ISO 1024. *International terminology standards—Preparation and layout*. Geneva, 1992.

Kahane, Howard. *Logic and Philosophy: A Modern Introduction*. California: Wadsworth Publishing Company, 1969.

Kipfer, Barbara Ann. *Workbook on Lexicography*. Exeter, England: A. Wheaton & Co. Ltd., 1984.

Landau, Sidney I. *Dictionaries: The Art and Craft of Lexicography*. New York: Charles Scribner's Sons, 1984.

Robinson, Richard. *Definition*. Oxford, England: The Clarendon Press, 1965.

Sager, M. Juan Carlos. "Definition in Terminology." In *Problèmes de la définition et de la synonymie en terminologie*. Québec: GIRSTERM, 1983.

# EXERCISES

1. Analyze the following context and formulate a definition for *flood current* and *ebb current* using the semantic features identified. State the method of definition you have chosen.

   To the geologist, tides are important because the rise and fall of water level sets in motion alternate landward and seaward flows of water in the entrances to bays and harbors, and in tidal streams. Such water movements are called tidal currents . . . . As tide level rises, a landward flow of water, the *flood current*, is set up; this usually continues strong until well after the water level has begun to fall. The current then comes to a standstill, the *slack water*, after which the flow sets in again, but in reverse, to become the *ebb current*, which moves the water back toward the open sea. The ebb current flows until well after low water, when it weakens and another slack water point is reached. So, about every six and a quarter hours there is a current opposite to the direction of the previous flow.

   (Source: Strahler, p. 58.)

2. Formulate a **definition by genus and difference** and a **partition definition** for the term *loom* using the context provided in Chapter 8.

# CHAPTER 12

# SYNONYMY

## 12.0 Typology of Synonyms

There are three types of synonyms in terminology: *real synonyms*, which represent the same concept and can be used interchangeably; *quasi-synonyms*, which represent the same concept but are used differently; and *pseudo-synonyms*, which belong to the same semantic field and thus share certain semantic features but are differentiated by their specific characteristics.

**Real Synonyms**

There are two main schools of thought on real synonyms. One asserts that real synonyms are found more frequently in the general language than in special languages and that the more specific the concept, the rarer real synonyms. The other maintains the opposite: that real synonyms are more common in special languages than in the general language. Whatever the case may be, real synonyms are, in fact, found in special languages. They can include:

(a) terms that represent different characteristics of a concept, e.g. *prepaid telephone card* and *long-distance telephone card* (telecommunications)

(b) terms that include the inventor's name as opposed to a characteristic of the concept, e.g. *Likert scale* and *summated scale* (statistics)

(c) terms that include different inventors' names, e.g. *Venn diagram* and *Euler diagram* (mathematics)

(d) borrowed terms as opposed to native terms, e.g. *col* and *pass* (geography)

(e) terms borrowed from Latin or Greek as opposed to English, e.g. *annulus* and *ring* (botany)

(f) terms that represent an emerging and evolving concept, e.g. *term* and *terminology unit* (terminology).

Variants of terms are also considered to be real synonyms despite the fact that they cannot always be used interchangeably. Variants include:

(a) syntactic variants, e.g. *point of origin* and *origination point* (broadcasting)

(b) morphological variants, e.g. *terminology unit* and *terminological unit* (terminology)

(c) spelling variants, e.g. *focused interview* and *focussed interview* (statistical surveys)

(d) ellipsis, e.g. *prepaid telephone card* and *phone card* (telecommunications)

(e) abbreviation, e.g. *CD* and *compact disc* (sound recording).

**Quasi-Synonyms**

As mentioned above, quasi-synonyms refer to the same signified, but the conditions under which they are used differ. *Film editing* and *film cutting* both refer to "creatively altering the originally recorded order or length of film material"; however, the former is frequently used, the latter rarely. *Dynamic microphone* and *moving coil microphone* both represent "a device operated by an electric coil and magnetized iron bar and used to transmit or record sound"; however, the former is used in the United States, the latter in Great Britain. *Cookie* and *gobo* both designate "an opaque shade used to screen a set light"; however, the former is jargon, the latter customary. Although these pairs of terms cover the same concept, they are differentiated by their frequency of use, geographic region of use, and register of language. As a result, they cannot be used interchangeably. The choice of appropriate term will depend on the communication context.

**Pseudo-Synonyms**

Pseudo-synonyms are terms that belong to the same semantic field and thus share a certain number of semantic features, but are differentiated by their specific characteristics. For example, *couch*, *sofa* and *loveseat* all refer to "an article of furniture, usually with arms and a back, designed to seat two or more people"—this is the semantic field they share. Nonetheless, they all have clearly distinguishing features: a *couch* can have only one arm and a partial back and be used for reclining; a *sofa* is a long seat which is often convertible into a bed; and a *loveseat* is a small sofa which usually seats only two people.

Pseudo-synonyms, in fact, are not synonyms at all, but rather terms that are often used equivocally by users who believe them to be synonymous. The terminologist's role in such cases is to clarify the similarities and differences by duly defining the concepts in question.

## 12.1 Establishing Synonymy

### 12.1.1 Real Synonyms

To determine whether two or more terms are real synonyms, the terminologist must confirm that they represent the same concept, bear no discrepancies in usage, and can therefore be used interchangeably. Real synonyms offer an important stylistic resource, even in special languages. Nevertheless, an abundance of real synonyms can hinder efficient communication by creating the impression that there is more than one concept involved.

### 12.1.2 Quasi-Synonyms

To establish quasi-synonymy, the terminologist must identify the concept covered and pinpoint discrepancies in usage. Differences in usage are generally context-conditioned and must be marked by usage labels.

**Sociolinguistic labels**: Sociolinguistic labels are used to indicate differences in level of language or register. For example, *coryza* and *head cold* refer to the same concept, but do not belong to the same register. The former is technical, the latter general. *Electrician* and *juicer* designate the same function in television production, but the former is customary, the latter jargon. *Valium* and *tranquilizer* cover the same concept, but cannot be used interchangeably: the former is a trademark, theoretically reserved for use by its owner, the latter a generic term.

**Geographic labels**: Different terms that refer to the same concept may be used in different geographic regions. For example, the person responsible for the artistic and technical design of a television program is called *producer* in Canada and *director* in the United States.

**Temporal labels**: Temporal labels are used to denote differences in terms over time. Terms are created, can gain acceptance, later lose ground, and ultimately disappear. When a term is first coined, it is considered a *neologism*; when its usage wanes, it is thought to be *outmoded*; and once it has disappeared from use, it is labelled *archaic*. For example, *chain* in the sense of "a group of radio or television stations linked by wire or radio relay" is outmoded and has been superseded by *network*. It should be noted, however, that a term designating a reality that no longer exists is not necessarily outmoded or archaic: *diddle bow* is not an outmoded term, but the designation of a rudimentary musical instrument that is no longer used.

**Profession labels**: Only terms that represent the same concept in a given subject field are considered synonymous. This is because terms are always studied in the context of the specific field in which they are used. Subject fields can, however, overlap and intersect. For example, the field of broadcast measurement includes both broadcasting and advertising terminology, since the ratings are established primarily for the purposes of advertisers. When broadcast measurement experts refer to "the total number of television viewers or radio listeners tuned to a station for all quarter-hour or reference periods considered", they speak of the *duplicated audience*; when advertisers refer to the same concept, they speak of *total impacts*. Such differences must be duly marked.

**Frequency labels**: Terms that represent the same concept are not necessarily used with the same frequency. For example, *split sponsorship* is used much less frequently than its synonym *cosponsorship*. *Casting director* is used more frequently than its synonym *talent director*.

Usage labels are not mutually exclusive. Obviously a term will never be frequently used and, at the same time, outmoded. But a term can certainly be outmoded and belong to a specific register, or be both outmoded and a regionalism.

### 12.1.3 Pseudo-Synonyms

Pseudo-synonyms are analyzed in two stages: the first consists in defining the semantic field shared by the terms in question; the second, in determining the specific characteristics which differentiate them. The semantic field of *chair*, *armchair* and *stool*, for example, can be defined as "article of furniture designed to seat one person", and the specific characteristics differentiating them as "back without arms" (chair), "back and arms" (armchair) and "no back or arms" (stool).

## 12.2  Studies of Synonyms

Differences between synonyms are indicated on terminology records; the source cited must, however, provide differentiating information. For example, the following synonymic context for *peigne* and *ros*, used in the field of textiles, identifies two points of usage: "Le peigne, encore appelé ros dans certaines régions, sert à rabattre la duite contre le tissu déjà constitué." "Encore" indicates that *ros* is outmoded in comparison with *peigne*, and "dans certaines régions", that it is a regionalism. These points of usage can be indicated on the record by means of usage labels.

If the source cited on the record does not contain differentiating information, the terminologist must conduct a study of the synonyms in question to define the concept covered and pinpoint any differences in usage. The following approach is suggested in conducting such studies.

### 12.2.1   Determining the Type of Synonym

Since there are three types of synonyms, the first step in conducting a study of synonyms is to determine the type involved. Sometimes groups of terms to be studied include more than one type. This must be ascertained at the outset.

## 12.3   Short Sample Studies

### 12.3.1   Real Synonyms

If the terms to be studied are real synonyms, the terminologist must prove that they cover the same concept, providing adequate sources, and determine that there are no peculiarities of usage.

Consider the terms *prepaid phone card*, *prepaid telephone card* and *phone card*, used in the field of telecommunications. The following text was selected from the documentation consulted:

> In 1976 the first prepaid phone cards were introduced in Europe. More recently they have been introduced in the United States. Frequently asked questions and answers about these cards are as follows:
>
> **What is a "phone card"?**
>
> The term "phone card" is an abbreviated description of what is actually a "prepaid telephone card". Phone cards are a convenient economical way to make long distance

phone calls. . . . A prepaid phone card is a type of debit card and represents phone time that has been paid for in advance. . . .

These . . . cards are inserted into specially designed public payphones which decrement the value of the card as it is used.[1]

This text provides sufficient information to define the concept, i.e. a card, purchased in advance, which allows the user to make long distance calls for a specified length of time from specially equipped payphones. It states that *phone card* is short for *prepaid telephone card*, indicates that it is short for *prepaid phone card*, and shows that the terms are used interchangeably in context.

A number of other documents from various sources were also consulted and confirmed that *prepaid phone card* and its two variants are used interchangeably and with similar frequency.[2]

### 12.3.2 Quasi-Synonyms

If the terms to be studied are quasi-synonyms, the terminologist must document the concept covered by each, then identify the differences in usage, providing appropriate supporting sources.

Take, for example, the term *prepaid phone card* above and two other synonyms, *prepaid telecard* or *telecard*. The context cited in 12.3.1 above provides enough information on *prepaid phone card* to define the concept it represents. Since *prepaid telecard*, like *prepaid phone card*, is a relatively new term, it does not yet appear in any general or specialized dictionaries. Some of the contexts found containing the term are as follows:

---

1. *Moneycard Collector Faq Page* appearing on the Internet, May 1996.

2. Numerous articles were consulted from business newspapers as well as newsletters and journals on phone cards, published primarily in the United States, but also in Canada, Europe, Australia and the United Kingdom, between October 1994 and January 1996.

> One of the hottest trends in telecommunications is the prepaid telecard. These cards work much like the telephone calling cards, except you pay in advance for a specific number of minutes. As you use the card, the number of speaking minutes is reduced. When the card is used up, you simply throw it away.[3]
>
> Loctite Corporation... launched a North American sweepstakes to promote its "No Loose Bolts" liquid threadlocking adhesive. Randomly-chosen retailers and consumers will be awarded a total of 2,100 prepaid phone card.... There will be 100 telecards worth 60 minutes of free phone time and another 2,000 cards worth 20 minutes of phone time. Prepaid phone cards were the perfect answer for the company's desire to do an out-of-the-ordinary promotion....[4]

These contexts suggest that *prepaid telecard* and *telecard* represent the same concept as *prepaid phone card*. They essentially indicate that *prepaid telecard* and its elliptical variant *telecard* refer to "a card, purchased in advance, which allows the user to make calls for a specified length of time". It can be assumed that the card is used for long distance, since it works like a calling card which is used strictly for toll calls. It can further be assumed that the calls are made from a payphone, since calls made from a user's home phone are automatically billed, not prepaid.

What these contexts do not show, however, is the difference between *prepaid phone card*, *prepaid telecard* and *telecard*. A number of sources were consulted[5] in an effort to ascertain any difference in usage. These sources indicate that *prepaid phone card* is much more frequently used than *telecard* and that *prepaid telecard* is very rarely used. Thus the difference among these synonyms is strictly a matter of frequency of use.

---

3. "Pre-paid Long Distance Calling Cards," *Tele Sales, Inc.*, The Internet, May 1996.

4. "Loctite Sticks to Phone-Card Sweepstakes," *Promo* VIII, 7: 14.

5. The articles referred to in footnote 1.

### 12.3.3 Pseudo-Synonyms

If the terms to be studied are pseudo-synonyms, the terminologist must show that they belong to the same semantic field, define the field on the basis of the semantic features they share, then pinpoint their specific characteristics.

Take, for example, the terms *prepaid phone card* and *calling card*. For *prepaid phone card* we can again refer to the context provided in 12.3.1 above. For *calling card*, we can consider the following context:

> In 1976 the first prepaid phone cards were introduced in Europe....
>
> **Are they the same as "calling cards"?**
>
> No, in fact they function in directly opposite ways. A prepaid phone card is a type of debit card and represents phone time that has been paid for in advance. On the other hand, a person making a long distance call with a calling card is actually using a credit card and thus is promising to pay the phone company at a later date.[6]

On the basis of this information, the semantic field shared by *prepaid phone card* and *calling card* may be defined as "a card which allows the user to make long distance calls when away from home". However, what differentiates the two is the fact that the *prepaid phone card* is purchased in advance and is used from public telephones; calls made with a *calling card* are billed afterward and can be made from any telephone outside the user's home, i.e. from a public or a private phone.

### 12.4 Conclusion

Real synonyms in special languages can offer an important stylistic resource. It would be difficult, for example, to draft a text—be it of a marketing, technical or statistical nature—on prepaid phone cards without being able to vary the

---

6. *Moneycard Collector Faq Page* appearing on the Internet, May 1996.

designation. Nonetheless, synonyms must be carefully studied in order to zero in on any differences and thus determine the appropriate expression to be used in a given context.

## BIBLIOGRAPHY

Duquet-Picard, Diane. *La synonymie en langues de spécialité: étude du problème en terminologie.* Québec: GIRSTERM, 1986.

Felbert, Helmut. *Terminology Manual.* Paris: Unesco, 1984.

*Problèmes de la définition et de la synonymie en terminologie.* Actes du Colloque international de terminologie, Québec: GIRSTERM, 1983.

## EXERCISES

1. Conduct a study of the following synonyms used in the field of textiles: *filling*, *picks* and *weft*.

2. Conduct a study of the following synonyms specific to the field of telecommunications: *telecommuter* and *teleworker*.

# CHAPTER 13

# TERM FORMATION

## 13.0 Introduction

*Term formation* is the creation of new designations or neologisms in special languages. Neologisms that spring from the minds of their inventors, with no prior history, are rare.[1,2] Rather, terms are created by adding new meaning to existing words, changing the morphology or grammatical class of established resources, and borrowing from other linguistic systems.

## 13.1 Characteristics of Contemporary English Term Formation

The characteristics of term formation vary from one subject field to another. In the biological sciences, where strict rules of nomenclature apply, classical derivation is favoured.[3] In the earth sciences, there is a relatively large degree of borrowing because geologists, mineralogists and meteorologists tend to accept terms for substances from the languages of the locales where they commonly occur.[4] In computer science, there is almost no borrowing because the early development of the field took place almost exclusively in English-speaking countries.[5]

---

1. A.L. Caso, "The Production of New Scientific Terms," p. 107.

2. "The stock example of . . . an 'original' word is *kodak*, which is said to have been manufactured by putting together letters very much as a bench might be made by putting together boards." (M.M. Bryant, *Modern English and Its Heritage*, p. 225.)

3. B.L. Raad, "Modern Trends in Scientific Terminology: Morphology and Metaphor," p. 128.

4. Caso, p. 107.

5. M.A. Covington, "Computer Terminology: Words for New Meanings," p. 66.

Be that as it may, certain generalizations can be made about modern English term formation as a whole.

### 13.1.1 Productive

English has a long history of enriching its vocabulary by creating new words. This is true not only of the general lexicon, but also of special languages. However, the current explosion of knowledge in almost every area of human endeavour—telecommunications, computer science, genetics, space exploration—has created an unprecedented need for the coining of new terms. Twentieth century scientists and innovators are making full use of the many resources available to augment their terminologies.

### 13.1.2 Preference for Composition and Metaphor

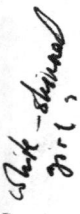

Composites—compounds and derived forms—were the chief source of new general-language words as long as ten centuries ago and remain the preferred process for adding to the general vocabulary.[6] Composites are also first in numerical importance as a source of new terms in special languages.[7] They offer many advantages, including potential precision and transparency, often enabling users to glean the meaning of a term from its component parts.

Metaphor and analogy, which have long been used to create terminology, are now receiving new attention. Not only do they offer the benefit of economy, but as Raad puts it,

> they use the very imprecision and suggestiveness of language to enhance communicative effectiveness . . . . Direct analogy between the genetic code and the alphabet, initially made because letters were used to classify gene types, has led to a series of effective terms in the field of genetics

---

6. J. Algeo, "Where do all the New Words Come From?," p. 270.

7. All the studies consulted indicate that composition is the predominant process of special-language term creation. The statistics they provide show that composites account for some 40 to 70 percent of all new terms, depending on the subject field.

which draw on the terms of an already established field: *morphology, punctuation, word, sentence, synonym, error* or *mistake, instruction, correction, marker, insertion,* and *deletion*.[8]

### 13.1.3 Tradition of Borrowing

English has a strong tradition of borrowing from almost all the languages it has come into contact with, for both general and special use.[9] Historically, English has borrowed primarily from Latin, Greek, French and German—languages which are strongly represented in law, medicine, science and technology. Today, it continues to tap foreign languages as a source of new terms.

## 13.2 Reasons for Creating Terms

### 13.2.1 Technical and Scientific Innovation

The primary reason for creating terms is to name the discoveries being made in so many fields of endeavour worldwide. New products and services are constantly being marketed, new devices fine-tuned, new diagnostic procedures developed and new cures found; the frontiers of knowledge are being pushed back in many different areas. Our need to communicate about these new realities creates the need to name them.

### 13.2.2 Changing Attitudes

New terms are also created to rename existing realities. Neologisms can reflect or encourage a change in attitude. For example, it was not until recently that people began speaking of the *Inuit* as opposed to the *Eskimo*, of *First Nations* as opposed to *Natives*. To attenuate the reaction of their workforce to personnel cuts, some companies talk of *rightsizing* rather than *downsizing*. To elevate the status of

---

8. Raad, p. 134.

9. J.C. Sager, D. Dungworth and P.F. McDonald, *English Special Languages: Principles and Practice in Science and Technology*, p. 284.

certain occupations which are not highly coveted, some organizations speak of *sanitary engineer* instead of *garbage collector*, *assistant* instead of *secretary*, *associate* instead of *clerk*.

### 13.2.3 Evolving Social Structures

Changes in the way we live and work spawn new terms. The *nuclear family* now coexists with the *single-parent family*, *same-sex couple*, *working mother*, and so on. The massive influx of women into the workplace has generated the need for the feminine form of some occupations and functions—*policewoman*, *chairwoman*, *businesswoman*—and the neutral form of sex-specific designations—*salesman* has given way to *sales representative*, *foreman* to *supervisor*, *anchorman* to *anchor*, *manpower* to *workforce*. The reorganization of the workplace itself has contributed new terminology: *teleworker*, *home-based business*, *home-office applications*, etc.

### 13.2.4 Need to Communicate Effectively

We create new terms to express ourselves more effectively. Phrases are lexicalized into compounds; *network for transmitting telephone signals* is compressed to *telephone network*. Compounds are reduced to their shortest possible form through clipping (*telecommunications company* to *telco*), abbreviation (*point of sale advertising* to *POS*), blending (*modulator/demodulator* to *modem*), acronymy (*radio detecting and ranging device* to *radar*) and initializing (*ultrahigh frequency* to *UHF*). Latin terms are replaced with English (*in law* instead of *de jure*, *in fact* instead of *de facto*), and popularized through metaphor: biology is replete with *maiden hair*, *lamb's ears*, *love-in-a-mist* and *forget-me-nots*.

## 13.3 Processes of English Term Formation

How are all the new terms created? Through four main methods: **semantic change**, in which an established word is given new meaning; **morphological change**, in which a term is formed by shortening an existing word or by joining existing words and formative elements; **conversion**, in which a term is coined by changing the grammatical class of an existing word; and by **borrowing** from other languages.

### 13.3.1 Semantic Change

Semantic change alters the meaning of an established word, but not its morphology or grammatical class. The processes of semantic change include adoption, expansion, metaphor, eponymy and metonymy.

#### 13.3.1.1 Adoption

Adoption changes the meaning of a word by giving it a new specific meaning, but one within its established general meaning. Adoption often accounts for terms that have been borrowed from one subject field by another or from the general language. Business management has drawn from the military nomenclature (*tactics, logistics, strategy, mission, target*), dentistry from civil engineering (*long-span bridge, abutment, mechanical retention*) and architecture (*arch, embrasure*), while computer science has borrowed from the general language (*read, write, memory, program, job*).

#### 13.3.1.2 Expansion

Expansion broadens the meaning of a word by giving it a new meaning, but one that bears little relation to its established meaning. Nuclear physicists have expanded the meaning of *dollar* to designate a certain quantity of atomic reactivity and *cents* to refer to the one hundred parts into which that quantity is divided.[10]

#### 13.3.1.3 Metaphor

Metaphor is a process by which a word is given a new meaning by analogy with its established meaning. Metaphors often use the names of animals, insects or body parts and

---

10. Caso, p. 104.

are based on analogy of form, function or position. *Crane* has been broadened to "a machine for raising and lowering heavy weights", *spider* to "a device consisting of a frame or skeleton with radiating arm or members", and *eye* to "a hole in the head of a needle" all by analogy of form; *horse* has been broadened to "a frame with legs used for supporting planks" and *fly* to "a fishhook dressed with feathers" by analogy of form and function; and *head* has been broadened to "the top of a screw" by analogy of position.

### 13.3.1.4 Eponymy

Eponymy is the widening of a proper name into a common noun. This process is frequently used in physics, where units of measure are commonly named after the inventor.[11] Examples include *ampere*, "basic unit of electrical current" (after French physicist André Ampère); *gauss*, "unit of magnetic induction" (after German mathematician Karl F. Gauss); *ohm*, "unit of electrical resistance" (after German physicist Georg Simon Ohm); and *watt*, "unit of electrical power" (after James Watt, Scottish inventor).

### 13.3.1.5 Metonymy

Metonymy is the use of the name of one thing for something with which it is closely associated. For example, *hard hat* (protective hat of a rigid material worn especially by construction workers) has, through association, acquired the meaning of construction worker. Such shifts in meaning include, but are not limited to, three main types of transfers.

(a) **The part for the whole or the whole for the part**: *col bleu* in French, like the example of *hard hat* above, is only one aspect of the clothing worn by blue-collar workers; through association with them, it has come to refer to the workers themselves. *Voice*, the essential attribute of singers, has through association come to designate singers themselves.

---

11. *Ibid.*

(b) **Concrete to abstract or abstract to concrete:** *technology*, "a technical method of achieving a practical purpose", has come to represent the actual equipment produced by such a method; *knowledge*, "the understanding of an art, science or technique", is used concretely to designate information in the term *knowledge worker*.

(c) **The material for the object:** *silver*, the metal, has come to designate table flatware made of silver; *glass*, a tumbler made of glass; and *china*, tableware made of china.

### 13.3.2 Morphological Change

Morphological change alters the form of an established word and, in certain cases, its meaning and grammatical class. The processes of morphological change include clipping and composition.

#### 13.3.2.1 Clipping

Clipping shortens the form of an established term, but does not change its meaning or grammatical class. There are various types of clipping, including hindclipping, foreclipping and midclipping.

In hindclipping, the most common type, one or more final elements of a term are omitted, resulting in *lab* from *laboratory*, *sync signal* from *synchronization signal*, and *sci-fi* from *science fiction*. In foreclipping, initial elements are omitted, resulting in *cello* from *violoncello*; in midclipping, the middle elements are dropped, resulting in *milliammeter* from *milliamperemeter*. Combined clipping is also found in some cases, such as *flu* from *influenza*.

#### 13.3.2.2 Composition

Composition includes all processes that join established words, affixes or combining forms to create new terms. This category includes affixation, compounding, combining, blending, acronymy and initializing.

### 13.3.2.2.1 Affixation or Derivation

In affixation, a prefix or suffix[12] is added to a stem[13] to form a new terminology unit.

**Prefixes**

There are two types of prefixes—free and bound. Free forms are words themselves and thus grammatically independent; bound forms are morphemes used in forming words and are grammatically dependent. Both can be attached to different parts of speech and serve to add a semantic feature.

(a) Free forms are generally function words—adverbs and prepositions. They retain their original meaning or acquire a new meaning when attached to a stem: *over* as an adverb refers to "in an excessive manner" and retains this meaning as a prefix in *overcompensation*; *out* as a preposition indicates "an outward movement", but has come to mean "in a manner that surpasses or excels" as a prefix in *outmanoeuvre*, for example. Free forms include *under* (lower than desired quantity) as in *underdose*; *over* (excessive) as in *overdose*; *anti* (opposing in effect) as in *antibacterial*; and *counter* (opposite) as in *counterclockwise*.

(b) Bound forms are generally of Latin or Greek origin. Some of the most commonly used can be categorized as follows:

**Negative, privative or reversative**: *a-* (not, without); *contra-* (against); *de-* (away); *non-* (not); *un-* (not). For example, *asynchronous, contraceptive, decarbonize, nonbiodegradable, untranslatable*.

**Temporal or sequential**: *ante-* (prior to); *pre-* (earlier than); *post-* (after); *re-* (again). For example, *antediluvian, prenatal, postproduction, rebroadcast*.

---

12. For a relatively complete list of affixes, see Sager, Dungworth and McDonald, pp. 295–300.

13. Word element which can be used as a term itself or as the base of a derivative (CSA Standard CAN/CSA-Z781-92, *Terminology—Vocabulary*, p. 7).

**Numeral**: *uni-* (one); *bi-* (two); *demi-* (half); *hemi-* (half). For example, *unicellular, bipolar, demifacet, hemisphere*.

**Locative**: *inter-* (between, among); *sub-* (under, below); *supra-* (over); *super-* (over, above). For example, *interstellar, submarine, supranational, superimpose*.

**Degree or size**: *hyper-* (excessively); *super-* (higher in degree); *sur-* (over, more); *ultra-* (beyond, more). For example, *hyperactive, superhuman, surtax, ultramicroscope*.

Prefixes are subject to semantic change like any other word or word element. As a result, many prefixes are polysemous; *in-*, for example, represents negation in *incommunicative* and penetration in *infiltration*; *de-* means remove in *dehydrogenate*, reduce in *deflate* and get off in *deplane*.

**Suffixes**

Suffixes are much more productive in special languages than prefixes. They alter the meaning of the stem or word to which they are attached and, in many cases, the grammatical class. Some of the most commonly used suffixes are as follows:

**Action or process**: *-ation* (action or process); *-fy* (invest with the attributes of); *-ing* (action or process); *-ment* (action). For example, *animation, gentrify, broadcasting, development*.

**Quality or state**: *-ance* (quality or state); *-ancy* (quality or state); *-ency* (quality or state); *-ence* (state); *-ification* (making); *-ity* (quality, state, degree); *-ous* (full of). For example, *protuberance, redundancy, transparency, interference, personification, luminosity, porous*.

**Agent**: *-er, -or* (one that performs); *-ant* (one that performs); *-ist* (one that operates a mechanical instrument). For example, *newscaster, translator, coolant, projectionist*.

**Instrument**: *-ive* (performs an action). For example, *explosive*.

**Collectivity**: *-age* (aggregate); *-ery* (aggregate); *-ing* (aggregate). For example, *wreckage, scenery, cabling*.

Suffixes, like prefixes, are subject to semantic change and can therefore be polysemous.

### 13.3.2.2.2  Compounding

Compounding joins two or more established words into a new terminology unit without otherwise altering their form.

Compounds are made up of two, three, or more word units in which the nucleus is determined by the modifier or modifiers. The relationship between nucleus and modifiers can be one of subordination (*radio station*), coordination (*bait-and-switch*), juxtaposition (*blue-green*) or disjunction (*on/off*).

The following examples provide an indication of the grammar of compounds:

**Compound nouns:**

adjective + noun = noun
e.g. *women's broadcast* (television production)

noun + adjective = noun
e.g. *stage right* (theatre)

verb + preposition + noun = noun
e.g. *fade to white* (television production)

adjective + adjective + noun = noun
e.g. *database management system* (information sciences)

adjective + preposition + adjective + noun = noun
e.g. *end-to-end network* (telecommunications)

noun + past participle + adjective + adjective + noun = noun
e.g. *fiber-based local area network* (telecommunications)

**Compound verbs:**

noun + verb = verb
e.g. *to air-condition* (building management)

noun + verb = verb
e.g. *to rustproof* (automative maintenance)

adverb + verb = verb
e.g. *to cross-reference* (library science)

verb + preposition = verb
e.g. *to log on* (information sciences)

**Compound adjectives:**

adjective + noun = adjective
e.g. *free-lance* (management)

noun + past participle = adjective
e.g. *computer-aided* (information science)

preposition + noun = adjective
e.g. *off-line* (information science)

noun + adverb = adjective
e.g. *user-friendly* (information science)

noun + preposition + noun = adjective
e.g. *step-by-step* (telecommunications)

noun + preposition + article + noun = adjective
e.g. *state-of-the-art* (telecommunications)

**Phrasal compounds:**

past participle + preposition + noun = participial phrase
e.g. *filmed on location* (television production)

preposition + article + noun = prepositional phrase
e.g. *on the air* (television production)

verb + article + noun = infinitive phrase
e.g. *to preempt a program* (television production)

noun + preposition + adjective + noun = nominal phrase
e.g. *request for copyright clearance* (television production)

### 13.3.2.2.3 Combining

Combining is the formation of words by joining those bound morphemes that *Webster's Third* calls *combining forms*, which are usually Greek or Latin, to other combining forms or words.[14] Examples include:

Greek combining form *penta* + Greek combining form *ode* = *pentode*

Greek combining form *auto* + Greek noun *chroma* = *autochroma*

Greek combining form *photo* + Latin noun *conductor* = *photoconductor*

Greek combining form *giga* + English noun *watt* = *gigawatt*.

### 13.3.2.2.4  Blending

Blending is a type of composition in which terms are created by uniting a word or word part with another word or word part. There are two main types of blending: simple and overlap.

In simple blending, the first word or initial syllables of the first word in a compound are joined with the last word or final syllables of the last word. For example, *newscaster* (news broadcaster), *simulcast* (simultaneous broadcast), *permafrost* (permanent frost).

In overlap blending, the antecedent words have common phonemes at the point of juncture, e.g. *modem* (modulator/demodulator).

### 13.3.2.2.5  Acronymy and Initializing

Acronymy and initializing both refer to the creation of a new term from the initial letters of a compound or phrase; acronyms, however, are pronounced as words, while initialisms are pronounced alphabetically. *STRAP* (simultaneous transmission and recovery of alternating pictures) and *radar* (radio detecting and ranging) are examples of acronyms;

---

14. Although some authors treat combining forms as affixes, there is an important distinction to be made: combining forms can be joined together to form a term, while affixes must be joined to a stem.

*LSI* (large-scale integration) and *AM/FM* (amplitude modulation / frequency modulation) are examples of initialisms; and *CD-ROM* (compact disc read-only memory) is a blend of the two.

### 13.3.3 Conversion

Conversion is a process in which a new term is created by changing the grammatical class of an established word—and necessarily its meaning—but not its morphology. Examples of conversion are as follows:

**Noun-adjective**: *knowledge* (understanding of an art, science or technique) refers to "information" in its adjectival form in *knowledge worker.*

**Noun-verb**: *photograph* (a picture or likeness) represents "the act of taking a picture" in its verbal form.

**Adjective-noun**: *preliminary* (something coming before or preceding something else) designates "a minor match preceding the main event" in its nominal form.

**Adjective-verb**: *empty* (containing nothing) means "to remove the contents of" in its verbal form.

**Verb-noun**: *refill* (to replenish) refers to "a product used to refill the exhausted supply of something" in its nominal form.

### 13.3.4 Borrowing

Borrowing includes processes that introduce into English words with no English antecedents. There are different types of borrowing: direct borrowing, adapted borrowing and loan translation.

In direct borrowing, a term is adopted from a foreign language with no modification. The terminology of classical ballet provides abundant examples: *plié, demi-plié, grand plié, demi-pointe, rond de jambe, relevé, tendu,* and so on.

In adapted borrowing, the spelling and pronunciation of the borrowed term are adapted to English, for example, *snorkel* from the German *Schnorchel*. This can include transliteration from languages that do not use the Roman alphabet, for example, *dim sum* (Chinese).

In loan translation, the components of a foreign-language word are literally translated into English. For example, *superman* from the German *Übermensch*.

### 13.3.5 Miscellaneous

There are two miscellaneous processes which are not particularly productive in special languages: back-formation and onomatopoeia.

**Back-Formation or Back-Derivation**

Back-formation is a process the reverse of affixation. In back-formation, a final element is removed from an established word to create a new term with a different grammatical class. A stock example is the verb *edit* which has been back-formed from *editor*.

**Onomatopoeia**

Onomatopoeic or echoic terms imitate the sound made by the object they represent. Examples of such terms include *blip*, *woofer*, *tweeter*, and *bleep*.

## 13.4  General Rules of Term Formation

General rules of term formation have been laid down by ISO in order to ensure the adequacy of newly formed terms. These rules are as follows:

**(a) Concision**

A term should be concise. If a term is too long, users will often shorten it for the sake of linguistic economy.

**(b) Linguistic Accuracy**

A term should comply with the morphological, orthographic, and phonetic conventions of the language in question.

**(c) Motivation**

A term should reflect insofar as possible the characteristics of the concept it represents.

**(d) Monosemy**

Ideally, a single term should be assigned to one concept, and one concept should be assigned to a single term.

**(e) Ability to Produce Derivatives**

A term should be able to provide derivatives.

## 13.5 Who Forms Terms?

In English special languages, terms are generally coined by the inventor of a new object or concept. The terminologist can be required to create new terms in certain circumstances, and is often called upon to collaborate with subject-field specialists in the term-formation process. Thus, it is essential for the terminologist to be able to devise new terms and to help others create new expressions.

# BIBLIOGRAPHY

Adams, Valerie. *An Introduction to Modern English Word-Formation*. London: Longman Group Ltd., 1973.

Algeo, John. "Where do all the New Words Come From?," *American Speech* 55 (1980): 264–276.

Bauer, Laurie. *English Word-Formation*. London: Cambridge University Press, 1983.

Bryant, Margaret M. *Modern English and Its Heritage*. 2nd ed. Toronto: Collier-MacMillan Canada, 1962.

Caso, Arthur Lewis. "The Production of New Scientific Terms." *American Speech* 55 (1980): 101–111.

Covington, Michael A. "Computer Terminology: Words for New Meanings." *American Speech* (1981): 66.

CSA Standard CAN/CSA-Z781-92. *Terminology — Vocabulary*. Toronto: Canadian Standards Association, June 1992.

Franks, Anne. *Neologisms in Computer Terminology*. Montréal, n.p., 1981.

Raad, B.L. "Modern Trends in Scientific Terminology: Morphology and Metaphor." *American Speech* 64, 2 (1989): 128–136.

Sager, Juan C. *A Practical Course in Terminology Processing*. Philadelphia: John Benjamins Publishing Company, 1990.

Sager, Juan C., David Dungworth, and Peter F. McDonald. *English Special Languages: Principles and Practice in Science and Technology*. Germany: Oscar Brandstetter Verlag KG, 1980.

## EXERCISES

1. Research the meaning and analyze the morphology of the following terms. Determine the process by which they were formed.

    *telecommuter* (telecommunications)
    *information highway* (telecommunications)
    *footprint* (satellite communications)
    *infomercial* (advertising)
    *near miss* (military)
    *ultrawide-angle lens* (television production)
    *luminosity* (television production)
    *talent* (television production)
    *to air* (television production)
    *mass media* (communications)

2. Evaluate the terms above using the general rules for term formation provided in 13.4.

# CHAPTER 14

# STANDARDIZATION

### CATHERINE A. BOWMAN

## 14.0 What are Technical Standards?

Technical standards are specifications or guidelines that outline safety or performance requirements for products, processes or services. Standards deal with a multitude of topics ranging from bicycle helmets and telecommunications equipment to quality assurance programs and the environment. They must be written in clear, precise, unambiguous language. Technical standards are widely used as references.

## 14.1 Scope of Technical Standards

Technical standards are produced at different levels: international, national or provincial, or by a given industry, company or professional association.[1]

Standards can be compulsory or voluntary. An example of a compulsory standard is the Canadian Electrical Code. Because it is cited in legislation, manufacturers of electrical products must comply with its requirements to sell their products in Canada. Noncompliance with compulsory standards may be penalized. Other standards are voluntary and may be used by a particular industry or profession as guidelines for quality or business conduct. The Canadian welding industry, for example, has produced a number of standards on welding safety, quality, inspection and French terminology. Compliance with voluntary standards is not enforceable other than by consensus of the interested parties or through consumers' refusal to buy products that do not meet the requirements of standards.

---

1. See Chapter 15, section 15.9.1, for the addresses of certain standards organizations.

## 14.2 Consensus

Standardization is a process that requires a consensus. Technical standards are generally developed by committees of subject-field experts who represent different areas of a particular field. Committee members must agree on the content and wording of the standard: this helps ensure that the various aspects of the subject are dealt with objectively.

## 14.3 Standards in the Field of Terminology

Some of the standards used in the field of terminology are listed below. ISO (International Organization for Standardization) Standard 10241 describes the information to be included in international terminology standards and how it is to be presented. Two other ISO standards, ISO 704 and ISO 1087, have been adopted as national standards in Canada (CAN/CSA-Z780 and Z781). They deal with the vocabulary of terminology as well as the principles and practices of the field.

| | |
|---|---|
| ISO 639:1988 | *Code for the representation of names of languages* |
| ISO 690:1987 | *Documentation—Bibliographic references—Content, form and structure* |
| CAN/CSA-Z780-92 | *Principles and methods of terminology* (ISO 704:1987) |
| CAN/CSA-Z781-92 | *Vocabulary of terminology* (ISO 1087:1990) |
| ISO 3166:1988 | *Codes for the representation of names of countries* |
| ISO 7154:1983 | *Documentation—Bibliographic filing principles* |
| ISO 10241:1992 | *International terminology standards — Preparation and layout* |

## 14.4 Linguistic Standardization

The purpose of linguistic standardization is to facilitate and expedite the communication of information. It is not meant to stifle creativity: the goal is simply to make the message easier to understand.

### 14.4.1 General-Language Standardization

General language is occasionally standardized to some extent by businesses that feel the need to control the quality of their internal documents and their correspondence with customers. Standard letter formats, writing rules, style guides, and document templates are used for this purpose. A more extreme example of general-language standardization is the use of controlled or simplified language in operation and maintenance instruction manuals written for customers. (Controlled language is usually introduced to facilitate machine translation of these texts. It can also target a particular readership, such as non-native language speakers.)

### 14.4.2 Special-Language Standardization

More often, special languages are standardized. Because terms are invented whenever there is a need to express a new concept, different designations may be given to the same concept in different geographic areas. In bygone days, some of these designations fell by the wayside over time, as one product achieved market dominance over its competitors, leaving one or two terms which were more frequently used.

Nowadays, however, this process of "natural selection" is outpaced. The rapid proliferation of scientific and technological developments has given rise to the creation of an unprecedented number of new terms, which are quickly disseminated through new communications and information technology. In some cases, the abundance of new terms can impede effective communication. Vague or inappropriate terminology has always been a nuisance for consumers, but the problem has become acute with the globalization of trade.

There can be no room for misunderstanding in international business contracts.

Terminology standardization in English is usually triggered by the need (1) to simplify expression by selecting one term from a number of synonyms; (2) to provide precise definitions of evolving concepts; or (3) to differentiate related concepts within a particular subject field.

These needs often become evident during technical standardization, when standardization committee members realize that they all have different opinions as to the meaning of a particular term used in their field.

Standardizers rarely create new terms in English: new terms are usually coined by the people who develop new concepts. This is not the case with other languages, however, where terms must often be invented for new concepts that are imported from other cultures.

English is so widely used as an international language that national standards in many countries are actually translations of English-language international standards. The English used in international documents should not reflect the usage of any one English-speaking community. Consequently, international terminology standards, like technical standards, are often adapted before they are adopted as national standards. This explains some of the terminological discrepancies between standards. An example of this is CAN/CSA Z243.58, *Information Technology Vocabulary*, published by the Canadian Standards Association. This standard is essentially a compilation of terms from ISO/IEC 2382, the international information technology vocabulary standard, but Canadian usage is listed first.

## 14.5 Who Standardizes Terminology?

Standardization must not be subjective or unilateral. An organization must be granted proper authority to develop standards. In the case of the *Office de la langue française* in Québec, for example, a mandate was conferred by law to standardize and enforce the use of standardized French terminology in public advertising in Québec and in all business dealings with the provincial government. Some official standards development bodies, such as the Canadian Standards Association and the *Bureau de normalisation du Québec*, produce voluntary terminology standards for use in Canada. At the international level, the International Organization for Standardization (ISO) and the International Electrotechnical Commission (IEC) are important producers of terminology standards. In this context, it is imperative to have precise terms and definitions which can be referred to when developing international standards in technical subject fields or when conducting international business transactions. Two examples of international terminology standards, both of which are updated on a regular basis, are ISO/IEC 2382 *Information Technology Vocabulary* and IEC 50 *International Electrotechnical Vocabulary*.

Some professional groups, such as the Canadian Institute of Chartered Accountants (*Terminology for Accountants, Dictionnaire de la comptabilité et de la gestion financière*), have been delegated the responsibility of standardizing the terminology used by their members or within their profession. Moreover, companies often find they need to standardize terminology for internal use and for communication with their customers, especially when they have several product lines or operations in different geographic locations.

Like technical standards, terminology standards are developed by committees whose members represent the various facets of a field: academia, business, government and consumers. Committees establish their own operating rules, based on guidelines provided by the standards development organization, so that their decisions are consistent. In terminology standardization, difficulties include how to deal with spelling variations, regional usages, synonyms, polysemous terms, and the criteria for acceptability of new terms.

Most terminology standardization in English is carried out by subject-field specialists rather than terminologists. As previously noted, the need to standardize terminology is often felt during technical standardization. Most technical standards include sections where some of the terms used in that particular standard are defined. Ideally, a glossary should be developed before the technical standards in order to clarify the conceptual framework and establish appropriate designations. More often, the glossary is compiled after a number of technical standards have been issued in an effort to collect, order and harmonize the terms used.

Subject-field specialists, because of their knowledge of their field and its specific concepts, are well placed to establish a nomenclature of terms, and generally know what information needs to be conveyed in a definition. A terminologist can expedite the terminology standardization process considerably by providing guidance in documentary and terminological research and methodology. The terminologist can further contribute by analyzing source documentation, organizing the concepts by means of tree diagrams, formulating definitions, and offering advice on techniques for coining new terms or selecting one preferred term from a number of synonyms.

## 14.6  Which Terms Need to be Standardized?

It is possible to standardize all the terms in a particular field. However, the time, effort and cost involved would be prohibitive, and the standard would likely be outdated before it was published. A selective approach, which concentrates on fundamental terms or problem areas, is more realistic. As previously mentioned, problems can include an abundance of synonyms for a given concept, confusion with regard to related concepts, ambiguity in existing definitions, inappropriateness of terms used, regional differences in usage, or the lack of a designation for a new concept.

## 14.7 Dissemination of Standardized Terms

The use of standardized terminology is rarely compulsory and depends on the goodwill of the users and the credibility of the standardizing organization. The best way to promote the use of standardized terms is to incorporate them into legislation, or into technical or industrial standards. These documents are widely circulated and are required reading for many people. The terms in them thus become familiar to all interested parties and are eventually used spontaneously because everyone understands them. Broadcasting through the media, on television or in newspapers, also has a major impact because of the wide audience reached. Key users are important as well: teachers, writers and specialized translators are excellent promoters of standardized terminology.

## 14.8 Terminology Standardization Process

The steps in terminology standardization are similar to those in subject-field research: determining the need, researching the documentation, developing and organizing the nomenclature, investigating the terms, selecting or drafting definitions, and so on. Standardization studies must be well-organized and thorough. The problems must be clearly stated, all the various arguments and possible solutions presented and tested, and a solution recommended. The files prepared for them must be coherent and logical so that all members of the standardization committee can judge the merits of the solutions.

Let's look at four types of problems requiring standardization, how these problems are dealt with, and how potential solutions are evaluated and treated.

### 14.8.1 Polysemous Terms

It is common for terms to have different meanings in different fields. The term *bridge*, for example, has one meaning in dentistry and another in civil engineering. This does not usually pose a problem unless one meaning is so common that it eclipses the other(s). Terms can also have different meanings within a given field or subfield. The term *picking*, for instance, has three different meanings in the field of textiles: harvesting cotton, snagging and weaving. This can cause confusion if the context is not absolutely clear.

In the case of polysemous terms within a subject field, all meanings should be noted, with appropriate supporting sources. The problems caused in communication should be described. The relationship between the various meanings should be analyzed and an inventory made of other terms that may be used instead.

The recommendation may be to maintain the multiple meanings with limited applications for each meaning, or to propose a specific term for each meaning, supported by logical arguments and sources.

### 14.8.2 Abundance of Synonyms

Standardization should not be considered a means of eliminating synonyms, as these are products of a healthy language and are a stylistic resource. Only when there are too many terms for one concept, or communication is complicated, should one term be given preference. Special languages need to be precise. Consider the context of international trade. Linguistic and cultural differences make communication difficult to begin with, so it is very useful to have clearly-defined standardized terminology to which all parties can refer. In this context, synonyms need to be minimized.

In studying this type of problem, the concept must first be properly defined and its essential characteristics noted. Each synonym must then be analyzed to determine whether it shares all the same characteristics. Deviating terms can be eliminated from the study. The way in which each term in the group is used must be verified (see Chapter 12, *SYNONYMY*), then the terms can be evaluated according to the following criteria.

**Frequency**: Language is essentially a matter of convention, so the frequency with which a term is used is very important. There is not always a scientific way to determine frequency. Automated documentation with concordancers or indexing software is not widely available, so often this criterion must be evaluated empirically by checking various reference works and dictionaries, asking users for their opinion, and so on. All other criteria being equal, the more frequent term should be preferred over its competitors. Frequency must not be considered only on a regional basis, however. For example, the term *nuisance ground*, meaning garbage dump, is used only in Alberta. Although this term is standardized at the provincial level as a result of its use in legislation, it is not a good candidate for national or international standardization.

**Usability**: The term should be as easy to use in speech and writing as possible. Concision, pronounceability and spelling are important considerations. Long paraphrasing and terms with multiple qualifiers complicate expression. A term is not a definition of a concept, but rather its label.

There is a widespread tendency in English to use acronyms and initialisms to compress lengthy terms. *Radar* (radio detection and ranging) and *modem* (modulator/demodulator), for example, are now accepted as terms and their long form is rarely used. This compression process can easily be taken too far, however. As a rule, short forms should not be standardized except as synonyms of the long form of a term.

The potential for derivation is another factor in usability. Can other parts of speech be formed with the term (e.g. *commuter, to commute, commuting, a commute*)? Can other terms be formed easily with the term (e.g. *commuting time, telecommuter*)?

**Adequacy**: Ideally, a term should represent only one concept in a field. In practice, this principle need not be followed too absolutely, as multiple meanings do not always cause confusion. Nevertheless, when comparing synonyms, the fact that one of them may have other meanings may be a reason not to standardize it.

Cases in which polysemy results from a shift in a term's meaning warrant special attention. The more natural the shift (see Chapter 13, *TERM FORMATION*, section 13.3.1), the more acceptable the multiple meanings are. Examples of logical shifts in meaning are *hardware* in general usage and in information technology, and *tissue* in medicine and in packaging. If the shift in meaning is arbitrary, however, the synonym should be discarded.

An example of a term that is woefully inadequate for standardization purposes is *cookie monster*. Borrowed from the name of a character in a popular North American children's television show, the term is used in computer security to designate a virus that is a nuisance but does not damage the computer files in which it lurks. This whimsical term has no clear relationship to the technical reality (see following paragraph on motivation), and its cultural ties also render it totally unsuitable for standardization. The standardized term for this concept is *benign virus*.

**Motivation**: A term is motivated if the concept it designates is obvious, either from its etymology, or from the meaning of its constituent parts. *Shade-tolerant tree* and *biodiversity* (short for *biological diversity*) are examples. Terms that comply with the morphological conventions of a language are often motivated. With time, motivation may become less clear and even completely obscured without the functional value of the term being affected. Many users can no longer see the etymological motivation of words formed from Latin or Greek (*diameter* and *excavator*, for example). The same is true of terms that have been in common usage for a long time.

*Blackboards* are now usually green or white. *Irons* are more likely to be made of stainless steel.

To sum up, the preferred term in a group of synonyms should be selected according to its usage and how it measures up against the aforementioned criteria.

### 14.8.3 Appropriateness

Sometimes a term is incorrectly used in a meaning other than that generally recognized, either because of an unfortunate shift in meaning (such as the term *hacker* in information technology) or because it is confused with related concepts. In such cases, the reason the term is not appropriate should be clearly established by comparing the accepted meaning with the contested one and by noting the meaning of the terms with which it is confused. The arguments should bring out the disadvantages of the improper usage and compare possible methods of rectifying the problem. The conclusion should recommend the best solution based on the arguments.

### 14.8.4 New Reality

A new object has just been invented and needs a name. It may already have been named in another language. Acceptance of the foreign-language term is called borrowing. As mentioned in Chapter 13, *TERM FORMATION*, English has a long tradition of borrowing as a means of enriching its vocabulary. When used indiscriminately, borrowing can be seen as a threat to linguistic integrity. This is rarely considered a problem in English; however, borrowing can pose difficulties if the adopted term is confused with an established English term or undergoes semantic change.

The first step in creating a new term is to define the concept in question. Possible labels can then be proposed, taking the criteria mentioned above into account, as well as the following one.

**Acceptability**: This is a psychological and social criterion. It is not always easy to predict users' reactions to a proposed term, but there are factors which frequently play a role in the rejection of a term. Pejorative or unpleasant associations, strangeness, or an overly scholarly effect (outside of scientific fields) may hinder acceptance of an otherwise excellent term.

## 14.9  Conclusion

Standards are very useful as reference. It is worth remembering, however, that like any other text, a standard is written for a particular public, be it international, national or local.

Because technical standards are widely consulted in industry, they have a strong influence on the terminology used by technical personnel. Terminology standardization, generally undertaken in response to specific needs, must be meticulously based on specific criteria, given its long-term and wide-ranging impact.

# BIBLIOGRAPHY

*ASTM Standardization News*, Volume 19, Number 12 (Special issue on ASTM Terminology Standardization). Philadelphia: American Society for Testing and Materials, December 1991.

*Consensus*. Ottawa: Standards Council of Canada. (Information magazine published eight times yearly.)

Sager, Juan C. *A Practical Course in Terminology Processing*. Philadelphia: John Benjamins Publishing Company, 1990.

# EXERCISES

1. Consider the various English equivalents for the French term *informatique* and evaluate the English term *informatics*. Should this term be standardized? Prepare a standardization study to justify your answer.

2. Do a synonym study of the following environment terms: *recycling, recovery, reuse* and *reclamation*. You will notice that they are used interchangeably in some contexts and that *recycling* is a polysemous term. What would be the impact of using these terms interchangeably in standards on environmental management and in environmental legislation?

3. Establish the relationship between the following terms and prepare appropriate standardization studies: *chipboard, fibreboard, particleboard, structural board, waferboard, oriented strandboard*. Use a tree diagram to show the relationships between these terms.

4. The word *hacker* originally referred to someone who was inexperienced or unskilled. Investigate its current meaning in the print media and in computer dictionaries. What has happened to the meaning of this word? How does the term *computer hacker* measure up against the criteria outlined in this chapter? What treatment for this term would you recommend to a terminology standardization committee?

# CHAPTER 15

# DOCUMENTATION

### CATHERINE A. BOWMAN

## 15.0 Introduction

The ability to locate, evaluate and make the maximum use of appropriate documentation is essential in terminology.

## 15.1 Documentation and Terminology

Today's language professionals are required to deal with a multitude of specialized topics. Terminologists are in the vanguard in this respect, and most of their time and energy is devoted to special languages: scientific, technical, administrative, or cultural. The efficacy of their work, however, always depends on the quality and relevance of the documentation they use.

Suitable documentation is extremely important because it is virtually impossible for terminologists to specialize. Term research can require forays into high finance, industrial processes, lawn furniture and flea collars, all within the same hour. In practice, therefore, terminologists must be very versatile and resourceful. Such quantum leaps can only be made successfully through the use of original-language documentation (texts which have not been translated) that is representative of the field in question. This documentation must clearly outline the concepts involved and express them in coherent terms which correspond to genuine usage in the field.

## 15.2 Documentation and Usage

To illustrate the terminological benefits of using original-language documentation, let's take a look at some terms extracted from French and English documents on sugar beets.

### 15.2.1 Terms Specific to Beet-Sugar Production

#### Cultivation

betterave sucrière = sugar beet
croisement = hybridization
démarier = to thin the beets
fanne = beet leaf
graine = seed (individual)
lit de semence = seed bed
passer le champ au cultivateur = to cultivate soil
semence = seed (collective)
semis de précision = space planting
semis dense = close planting

#### Harvesting

arrachage = lifting
décolletage, étêtage = topping
décolleter = to top
décolleteuse = topper (machine)
ramasseuse = harvester (machine)

#### Sugar Production

amorcer la cristallisation = to seed a liquid for crystallization
betteraverie, raffinerie = sugar factory; beet-sugar factory
carbonatation = carbonation
concentration = evaporation
coupe-racines = beet cutter; salad-maker
grainage = seeding
graine = seed crystal
jus clair = clear juice
jus de diffusion = raw juice
jus sucré = sweet juice
masse cuite = massecuite; fillmass
non-sucres (n. m. pl.) = non-sugar substances
pipette = proof stick
poste de pesée = scale

raffinerie, betteravere = sugar factory; beet-sugar factory
raffineur = sugar-boiler (person)
sucrier = sugar-maker (person)
trommel de diffusion = diffusion cell

One of the most striking aspects of this comparison is the difference between the French and English terms. Only a few of the terms could have been translated literally: *lit de semence = seed bed, jus sucré = sweet juice,* and *jus clair = clear juice*. An unverified literal translation would result in a pseudo-language that would be very confusing and misleading for the reader. Only by using adequate documentation to research authentic terminology can such pitfalls be avoided.

## 15.2.2 Differences: Synonyms, Register and Perspectives

The sugar-manufacturing facility can be called either *betteraverie* or *raffinerie* in French: one term specifies the product being processed (beets) and the other the principal operation (refining). Both terms are rendered in English by *sugar factory* or *beet-sugar factory*. Similarly, the abstract *semence* and the concrete *graine* in French are both *seed* in English.

*Salad-maker* is an informal English synonym for *beet cutter*. In French, there is no difference in register as only one term is used: *coupe-racines*.

The French term *croisement* refers to the operation used by botanists to create new varieties of plants. In English, the scientific term *hybridization* is preferred.

The operation for removing excess water from the raw juice is called *evaporation* in English and *concentration* in French. This is an example of a cause-and-effect relationship.

This short study illustrates why it is essential to use original-language documentation to obtain true-to-life terminology. Systematic recourse to literal translation or paraphrasing, so frequent in translation, produces a result that is totally unrepresentative of the target language and that can be very misleading. Language specialists therefore need access to original texts in the languages in which they work.

## 15.3 Available Resources

The computer revolution has given rise to the information revolution. Today, documented information of all kinds is more readily available than ever before. The challenge is no longer where to find documentation that appears to exist only in some inaccessible location, but to sift through mountains of irrelevant information to find the facts you really need.

### 15.3.1 Libraries

Public and institutional libraries are gold mines of information. For practicing terminologists, it may be difficult to visit these libraries during office hours. Interlibrary loans are a practical solution to this problem. Some companies also accept visitors to their libraries. Be sure to obtain permission first.

Larger libraries now have on-line indexes which make it much easier to locate a specific book or develop a list of potential references. Some of these index databases are accessible via the Internet, so you can consult them without leaving your office.

### 15.3.2 Existing Terminology Studies

Terminology studies have already been carried out in a number of fields. If they are based on sound methodology and reliable documentation, it is senseless to redo the work. Many low-cost vocabularies and glossaries have been published by the federal and provincial government language services, some large companies and associations, the United Nations, the European Union, and so on. A good number of other serious terminology studies are also available. They are there to be used.

### 15.3.3  Databases

Terminology reference material includes terminology banks. Access to these banks is essential, not only for the terms they contain, but for the sources they use and related bibliographic information. **Termium**, the *Banque de terminologie du Québec* and **Eurodicautom** are among the best-known terminology banks.

There are now many documentation databases. Some provide bibliographic references and others full texts. Bibliographic databases are useful for locating books and articles for subject-field research. University library indexes can be used as bibliographic databases and accessed via the Internet. Textual databases can provide the actual documents, either as photocopies or in a machine-readable format.

There are documentation databases in many fields: engineering, law, medicine, etc. They are generally accessible by direct subscription, on CD-ROM, via the Internet, or through large libraries. For the ordinary user, the principal way to access documentation databases is through large libraries.

### 15.3.4  Internet

Search engines such as Yahoo, Alta Vista, Magellan, Lycos and Web-Crawler can point you to the World Wide Web (www) pages of companies that sell particular products, or to information or documentation databases (such as standards) that may be accessible by subscription (paid or free). Language sites such as terminology banks, multilingual vocabularies, thesauri and general dictionaries are available to those who are on-line. Electronic bulletin boards can be a very useful means of obtaining answers to specific questions and often provide access to otherwise inaccessible technical specialists.

### 15.3.5 Electronic Media

Among the dictionaries and encyclopedias available on CD-ROM are the *Oxford English Dictionary*, *Encyclopaedia Britannica*, *Robert électronique*, *Petit Robert*, *Grolier Encyclopedia*. Nation-wide telephone directories may also be useful for checking company names, etc. Also available on CD-ROM are text corpuses of newspapers in which key words can be used to find information. Note that such information may be factual or linguistic.

## 15.4 Evaluating Documentation

Once you have found documentation on your topic, how do you assess its relevance? There are a number of factors to consider. What kind of information does it contain? Manuals and teaching materials are far more useful to terminologists than philosophical treatises because the former explain the concepts discussed while the latter do not. When was the documentation written and how essential is it to have up-to-date information on your topic? What are the author's credentials? For whom was the text written and why? Read the introduction and preface of reference materials to find answers to these questions. Also, on what is the information based: on recent studies, the author's experience? What research methodology did the author use? How is the information presented? Is there a bibliography or an index? Are there cross-references in the case of a glossary? Are there illustrations? Read a page or two. Is the text clear and understandable?

Remember that where you look for information depends on what you want to find. Advertisements in technical magazines may have the terms you need and even helpful pictures.

## 15.5 Terminology Reference Library

Two objectives should be kept in mind when setting up a terminology reference library. First, it must meet the requirements of terminological research by including appropriate subject-field documentation in addition to general-language references. Second, it must provide users of the library with efficient solutions to their terminology problems.

### 15.5.1 Terminological Research Requirements

For terminological research, original documents in each working language are required in all relevant subject fields. This documentation should include manuals, reports, handbooks, as well as technical standards[1] and internal documents such as job descriptions, maintenance instructions, etc., depending on the library's fields of activity. Remember that original documents, not translations, are required to find authentic terminology confirmed by characteristic usage. Translations offer no such guarantees. Texts must be representative of the field of study. They must reflect current general usage in the field, not just local or in-house usage. They must be well-written and express the ideas in a coherent, logical manner. Ideally, these references should be indexed in a subject file. If they are not, terminologists should make maximum use of tables of contents and indexes in the documents. Computerized databases simplify access: the financial outlay required in some cases is justified if the databases are consulted frequently. Also, more reference libraries are being computerized to optimize access to their documentation.

Manuals, reports and handbooks show terminology in its own environment. But since special languages are, to a large extent, subsystems of general language, standard general and specialized unilingual dictionaries are also required in a terminology reference library. *Webster*, *Random House*, *Oxford*, *Gage* and *American Heritage* are titles to be considered.

---

1. Technical standards, as described in the chapter on standardization, are useful sources of standard technical terminology.

Relevant unilingual, bilingual, or multilingual glossaries, vocabularies and terminology studies are the next documents to be considered, as there is no reason to redo research that has been well done by someone else. Quality control is a must, however. What sources and methodology were used? How is the information dealt with and presented (synonyms, cross-references, polysemous terms, etc.)? Access to the major terminology databanks should also be provided in a terminology reference library.

The result of all terminological research should be saved in a terminology file, be it a card file or a computerized database. In addition to saving time, this will help standardize usage, prevent duplication of effort and ensure that the information is valid and up to date.

For a card file, the filing system should be as simple and straightforward as possible. Alphabetical order is best, with cross-reference cards for all synonyms and equivalents in other languages.

For computerized terminology files, the database should be defined so as to allow the greatest possible flexibility when it comes to querying.

### 15.5.2 Users

Terminology reference libraries are often consulted by translators, writers and other users, in addition to terminologists. These people usually have a specific terminology problem to solve and want to do so quickly. The terminology file, banks and other references should be easy for them to find and use. The location and layout of the library should take this into consideration.

### 15.5.3 Classification System

Large libraries generally use the Library of Congress and/or Dewey decimal classification systems. These tend to be rather unwieldy for a small collection. Smaller libraries often adopt an in-house system based on their fields of specialization. Subject-field trees can be used to establish logical groupings that can often be applied to both documentation and terminology records. Here is an example:

**SUBJECT-FIELD TREE**

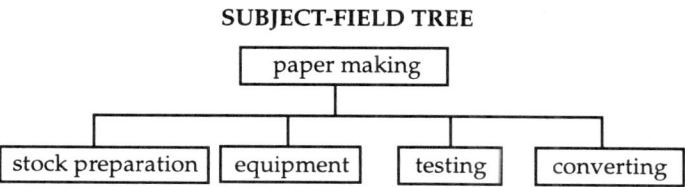

If needed, secondary subfields can be added as well. For example, equipment could be subdivided into pumps, paper machine, dryers, winders, coaters, sheeters, slitters and wrappers.

Access to information can be improved immensely by computerizing the author, title and subject indexes. As with terminology files, index databases should be designed for flexibility. A descriptor field containing key words selected from tables of contents, for instance, makes it easy to retrieve valuable information from documents that would otherwise be overlooked.

## 15.6 Documentalist

A reference library needs an administrator. The documentalist's primary function is to make life easier for the library users. In smaller libraries, such as a company translation department's documentation centre, the terminologist is often the documentalist as well.

The person responsible for managing a terminology reference library should have a solid background in library science, obtained either through education or experience. Other requirements are good interpersonal skills, curiosity, imagination, resourcefulness, and the ability to understand the essence of a terminology problem and the type of solution required.

Contacts with other libraries and a list of specialists who can be consulted should be developed.

### 15.7 Corpus

The following types of references should be included in a terminology reference library. Examples are provided for English and French.

#### 15.7.1 General Language References

(a) **General dictionaries**: *Webster's Unabridged, Random House, American Heritage, Gage Canadian Dictionary* and the most recent edition of *Webster's Collegiate Dictionary* or the *Shorter Oxford*. *Grand Robert de la langue française* (nine volumes, also available on CD-ROM), *Grand Dictionnaire encyclopédique Larousse* (ten volumes), *Trésor de la langue française* (contains lots of examples).

(b) **General Encyclopedias**: *Encyclopaedia Britannica, Encyclopedia Universalis*.

(c) **Style-related references**: *Webster's New Dictionary of Synonyms, The Synonym Finder* (J.D. Rodale), *Roget's Thesaurus, Random House Word Menu* (Stephen Glazier), Frederick Wood's *English Prepositional Idioms, The Canadian Style, The Chicago Manual of Style, Fowler's Modern English Usage, Harper's Dictionary of Contemporary Usage, A Comprehensive Grammar of the English Language* (R. Quirk et al.). The most recent editions of the *Petit Robert* and *Petit Larousse, Multidictionnaire* (de Villers), *Nouveau Dictionnaire des difficultés du français moderne* (Hanse), *Dictionnaire des difficultés de la langue française* (Thomas), Répertoire des avis linguistiques (Office de la langue française), Société Radio-Canada records, *L'Art de conjuguer* (Bescherelle), *Le Bon Usage* (Grevisse), *Le Guide du rédacteur, Le Ramat de la typographie* or *Code typographique*.

(d) **Bilingual Dictionaries** (English-French, French-English): *Robert-Collins* (Super Senior in two volumes), *Harrap's New Standard French and English Dictionary* (four volumes).

### 15.7.2 General Administrative References

(a) **Unilingual**: *Black's Law Dictionary, Barron's Business Guide dictionaries, Canadian Business Handbook* (very useful for correspondence, forms of address, meeting procedure). *Le français, langue des affaires* (Clas and Horguelin), *Le français au bureau* (Office de la langue française).

(b) **Bilingual**: *Dictionnaire de la comptabilité et de la gestion financière* (Ménard), Terminology Bulletins, vocabularies and lexicons published by the federal government and the Office de la langue française, *Dictionnaire juridique* (Quemner).

### 15.7.3 General Technical References

(a) **Unilingual**: *McGraw-Hill Encyclopedia of Science and Technology, Van Nostrand's Scientific Encyclopedia, McGraw-Hill Dictionary of Scientific and Technical Terms. Dictionnaire des industries* (Conseil international de la langue française), *Encyclopédie internationale des sciences et des techniques* (10 volumes, Les Presses de la cité), *Techniques de l'ingénieur* (various series on specific fields can be purchased separately: updates are provided by annual subscription).

(b) **Bilingual** : *Dictionnaire général de la technique industrielle, tome IX français-anglais, tome X anglais-français* (R. Ernst).

### 15.7.4 Specialized Documentation

Depending on the subject fields, this part of the collection should include specialized unilingual glossaries and any existing bilingual vocabularies. Laws, regulations and standards should be next, then manuals, collective agreements, catalogues, specialized monographs such as handbooks or textbooks, and trade journals. Many of these are accessible by computer in databases, on CD-ROM, or via the Internet.

## 15.8 Evaluating References

Before purchasing a new acquisition, its quality and scope should be assessed. If the book is widely known and used, its value may be obvious. If it is new, however, it should be carefully examined.

### 15.8.1 Dictionaries and Vocabularies

Read the reviews of dictionaries and vocabularies in trade journals. They generally give an overview of the content and a general evaluation which may provide the following information:

**Evaluation Criteria**

**Methodology**: Look at the bibliography (what sources were used, who wrote them, where and when, were original-language sources used?); how synonyms are dealt with (usage labels and cross-references); and how polysemous terms are handled (meanings clearly differentiated). Are the definitions clear?

**Structure**: Foreword (outline of the methods used); notes on the fields and subfields; index of any terms not listed in alphabetical order.

**Presentation**: Are codes and symbols explained? Are typographical conventions coherent?

**Nomenclature**: Check entries at random to see whether they are relevant to the field.

**Date of publication**: This may be more or less important, depending on the field.

### 15.8.2 Other Documents

**Opinion of Subject-Field Specialists**

Before buying a manual, handbook or other similar reference, ask the opinion of a specialist who already understands the requirements of terminology. Such a person can often provide information about the author and indicate whether the terminology used is representative.

**Other Criteria**

**Language**: Texts should be in the original language and should be well-written.

**Origin**: Check where the book was written to avoid problems with regional usage.

**Publication date**: Ensure that the information is still current.

### 15.8.3 Documentation of a Temporary Nature

This category includes advertising (catalogues, flyers, data sheets, etc.), current magazine articles and periodicals.

The same evaluation criteria apply to these documents, particularly those regarding the quality of the writing, the publication date and the sources used.

## 15.9 Useful Addresses

Note: Internet addresses tend to change frequently.

### 15.9.1 Standards-Writing Organizations

American National Standards Institute (ANSI)
11 West 42nd Street
New York, N.Y.
10036 U.S.A.
Tel.: (212) 642-4900
http://www.ansi.org

American Society for Testing and Materials (ASTM)
1916 Race Street
Philadelphia, Penn.
19103 U.S.A.
Tel.: (215) 299-5400
http://www.astm.org

Association française de normalisation (AFNOR)
Tour Europe
Paris La Défense Cédex 7 F-92049
France
Tel.: 33 (1) 42 91 55 55
http://www.afnor.fr

British Standards Institution (BSI)
389 Chiswick High Road
London W44 AL
United Kingdom
Tel.: +44 (0) 181 996 9000
http://www.bsi.org.uk

Bureau de normalisation du Québec (BNQ)
333, rue Franquet
Sainte-Foy (Québec)
G1P 4C7
Tel.: 1-800-386-5114 or (418) 652-2238
http://www.criq.qc.ca/bnq

Canadian Standards Association (CSA)
178 Rexdale Boulevard
Rexdale, Ontario
M9W 1R3
Tel.: (416) 747-4044
http://www.csa.ca

Deutsches Institut für Normung (DIN)
Burggrafenstraβe 6
D-10787 Berlin
Germany
Tel.: +4930/2601-1
http://www.din.de/frames

European Committee for Standardization (CEN)
Rue de Stassart 36
B-1050 Brussels
Belgium
Tel.: +32 2 550 0811
http://tobbi.iti.is/cen

Institute of Electrical and Electronics Engineers, Inc. (IEEE)
345 East 47th Street
New York, N.Y.
10017-2394 U.S.A.
http://www.ieee.org

International Organization for Standardization (ISO)
Central Secretariat
1, rue de Varembé, Post Office Box 56
CH–1211 Geneva 20
Switzerland
Tel.: +41 22 749 0111
http://www.iso.ch

International Electrotechnical Commission (IEC)
Central Office
3, rue de Varembé, Box 131
CH-1211 Geneva 20
Switzerland
Tel.: +41 22 919 0211
http://www.iec.ch

Standards Council of Canada (SCC)
45 O'Connor Street, Suite 1200
Ottawa, Ontario
K1P 9Z9
Tel.: (613) 238-3222
http://www.scc.ca

### 15.9.2 Terminology Research Organizations

Comité de linguistique
Société Radio-Canada
C.P. 6000, Succ. A
Montréal (Québec)
H3C 3A8

Comité d'étude des termes techniques français
11, avenue du Général-Pershing
Versailles 78000
France

Conseil international de la langue française
11, rue de Navarin
75009 Paris
France
Tel.: 33 1 48 78 73 95

Office de la langue française du Québec
200, chemin Sainte-Foy
Québec (Québec)
G1R 5S4
Tel.: (418) 643-2134

Translation Bureau
Public Works and Government Services
Ottawa, Ontario
K1A 0M5

### 15.9.3 Other Useful References

Canada Institute for Scientific and Technical Information (CISTI)
National Research Council of Canada
Building M-55, Montreal Road
Ottawa, Ontario
K1A 0S2
1-800-688-1222 or (613) 993-1600
http://www.cisti.nrc.ca/cisti/cisti.html

Eurodicautom
http://www.uni-frankfurt.de/~felix/eurodicautom.html
Telnet echo.lu

Ordre des traducteurs et interprètes agréés du Québec (OTIAQ)
2021 Union, Suite 1108
Montreal, Quebec
H3A 2S9
(514) 845-4411 or 1-800-265-4815
http://www.otiaq.org

International Federation of Translators (FIT)
http://umn.ac.be/atim/fit/index.html

Translator's Home Companion
http://www.lai.com/lai/companion.html

Canadian Permanent Committee on Geographical Names (CPCGN)
Geomatics Canada
National Resources Canada
615 Booth Street, Room 650
Ottawa, Ontario
K1A 0E9
Tel.: (613) 992-3405
http://ellesmere.ccm.emr.ca/cgndb/english/cpcgn.html

# BIBLIOGRAPHY

*Dewey Decimal Classification and Relative Index*. Albany: Forest Press.

Gorman, Michael and Paul. W. Winkler, ed. *Anglo-American Cataloguing Rules*. 2nd ed. Ottawa: American Library Association and Canadian Library Association, 1988.

Kohl, David F. *Acquisitions, Collection Development and Collection Use. A Handbook for Library Management*. Santa-Barbara: ABC-CIO, 1985.

Kohl, David F. *Cataloging and Catalogs. A Handbook for Library Management*. Santa-Barbara: ABC-CIO, 1986.

Osborn, Jeanne. *Dewey Decimal Classification. 20th edition. A Study Manual*. Colorado: Libraries Unlimited, Inc., 1991.

Whitely, Sandy, ed. *American Library Association Guide to Information Access: A Complete Research Handbook and Directory*. New York: Random House, 1994.

## ISO Standards on Documentation and Information

| | |
|---|---|
| ISO 5127 | *Documentation and information—Vocabulary* (several parts) |
| ISO 690 | *Documentation—Bibliographic references—Content, form and structure* |
| ISO 2108 | *Documentation—International standard book numbering* (ISBN) |
| ISO 3297 | *Documentation—International standard serial numbering* (ISSN) |
| ISO 5963 | *Documentation—Methods for examining documents, determining their subjects, and selecting indexing terms* |
| ISO 7275 | *Documentation—Presentation of title information of series* |

| | |
|---|---|
| ISO 639 | *Codes for the representation of names of languages* |
| ISO 3166 | *Codes for the representation of names of countries* |
| ISO 4217 | *Codes for the representation of currencies and funds* |

# EXERCISES

1. Visit your computer software store or a library and make a list of encyclopedias available on CD-ROM or diskette. Read the information on the package to find out who the targeted readers are (age group, etc.) and what is required to use them (hardware, software, etc.). If you can consult them, at a library, for example, consider how much factual content is really provided. Pictures can be very useful to terminologists but piano concertos are less so (unless you are having a stressful day).

2. List and compare the different types of documents you might use to conduct subject research in information technology and forest products. What criteria would you use to select documentation for these two fields? How would you rate the importance of each criterion (i.e., *essential, very important, useful but less important*)?

3. Compile documentation for a particular topic that interests you, such as cycling, construction of a wood-frame home, the stock market, the environment.

4. Evaluate some periodicals available on the newsstands or at the public library, such as *Canadian Business, Ecodecision, PC Magazine, Scientific American, Harvard Business Review*. Would they be useful for terminological research? If so, for what type of research? Why?

# CHAPTER 16

# TERMINOLOGY AND THE COMPUTER

ANDY LAURISTON

## 16.0 Introduction

Information processing has been used in terminology since the mid-sixties. At that time, large-scale specialized databases, known as *term banks*, were developed for storing and disseminating terminological data. From those beginnings, modern software systems have emerged for building, operating and maintaining terminology files of any size. Integration of these files with machine-aided translation (MAT) systems through an interface devised jointly by MAT experts and terminologists is a distinct prospect. Experimental systems for automating the terminologist's own job are now being tested and actually implemented, e.g., the terminology workstation used by the Department of the Secretary of State of Canada.[1]

## 16.1 Term Banks

Term banks are databases specially designed to store terminological information and make it available to subscribers, who either access a host computer or purchase a compact disc (CD-ROM). These very large-scale banks, which contain hundreds of thousands of records, are now tolerably user-friendly and have become indispensable to users of terminology.

The basic unit of information in term banks is the terminology record, which must meet recognized criteria for validity, i.e. information attested to by reliable sources, meaningful citations, and classification by field and subfield. Records can be accessed by any of a number of keys. The most widely

---

1. C. Leonhardt, "LATTER, the terminologist's workstation."

used key is the terminological unit, either in whole or in part, in all the languages used. For subject-field research, the ability to query by field or subfield is exceedingly useful. Access by just part of a terminological unit is another particularly valuable feature. When the user cannot find the answer to a query directly, a plausible, if unattested, solution can then be found by piecing together the results of a series of subqueries. For example, suppose a user wants to find the French equivalent for *capital asset pricing model*. If the full term cannot be found, the term can be broken down into such constituents as *capital asset, asset pricing, pricing model* and *pricing,* and the equivalents for the constituents can be used to infer an equivalent for the original term. This approach requires of the user a fair knowledge of the relevant subject field. The same requirement applies to a user when querying working records for which the concept is underspecified and only a proposed equivalent is given, or *full text* term banks in which all fields on a record, citations included, are indexed.

For translators, terminologists and other professional communicators, the quantity of information provided is often of more importance than the quality. They are usually able to separate the wheat from the chaff and even turn the chaff into palatable solutions to a particular communications problem.

Term banks can be accessed over telephone lines from a microcomputer or terminal equipped with a modem. Consulting them generally requires paying a time-sensitive usage fee over and above the subscription fee. To avoid the cost and inconvenience of remote access (congestion during peak hours), some banks are now being made available to subscribers on CD-ROM (compact disc read-only memory). New editions are distributed periodically to subscribers for an appropriate fee. A single disc can hold the entire contents of a large term bank, and can be read using a special drive. Users can consult several banks and dictionaries either from a dedicated microcomputer with multiple CD-ROM drives or from their own workstation linked to a server over a local area network (LAN).

Needless to say, term banks must pay for themselves by offering up-to-date information for a wide range of subject fields. Hence, teams of competent terminologists must continually add new records, enriching the terminological content through their work. Failing this, computerized term banks will be subject to the same criticism often leveled against printed publications—obsolescence.

## 16.2 Terminology File Management Systems

Term banks have not eliminated the need for personal or departmental terminology files to meet specific needs. Until recently, such files were compiled manually on index cards arranged alphabetically and accessible only by their entry terms. The microcomputer has given rise to automatic terminology file management systems for flexibly maintaining and sharing personal files.

Before computerizing a terminology file, the users of the file must be clearly identified, a rough estimate of the ultimate size of the file made, and the desired access and management features established. These specifications provide criteria for determining the software package to be used and the platform on which it can run.

Whatever type of file is to be computerized, the chosen package should offer certain features related to input, data transfer, querying, and record and file structure.

### 16.2.1 Ease of Input

It should be easy to input data. Easy input is less error-prone. Furthermore, simple procedures mean that the input operation can be carried out by an operator supervised by the terminologist. This is particularly valuable if the file being computerized contains a large number of records that do not require fundamental modification. The input program should allow for a spelling check so that typing mistakes, which can make useful information irrecoverable, are avoided. Validity checks should also be provided to ensure that all mandatory fields are filled with appropriate information, as defined by the terminologist in charge.

### 16.2.2 Import Facilities

Easy input should be accompanied by easy import. In other words, it should be possible to load information into the terminology file management system from another system, e.g. another database or a word processing system.

### 16.2.3 Query Facilities

Query facilities should give the user maximum access to the information stored. They should also enable the user to query records by all terminological units, including abbreviations and synonyms, and all constituents of complex terms, in all the languages used. Domain-specific processing requires query facilities by the record's subject field and subfield. A good file system should provide selective access by specifying several search criteria in a single query, e.g. all terms containing the word "rate" on records for the subject field of finance entered since 1990.

### 16.2.4 User Friendliness

It is also important that the file system be user-friendly, i.e. that the user be able to navigate easily through the system. Experience has shown that terminology files requiring extensive user training often go unqueried. A streamlined, intuitively-grasped query procedure is thus highly desirable. The ability to restrict the initial display to a list of entry terms, perhaps accompanied by the subject field, can also help the user navigate during the query session.

### 16.2.5 Structural Flexibility

The record and file structure should be flexible and adaptable. Field length should be variable to allow for long citations, complex terms with many modifiers, complex sources, and other needs that might arise unexpectedly. Some fields should be repeatable, so that the terminologist is not limited, say, to a fixed maximum number of synonyms or sources. Empty fields should not take up disc space. The file structure should allow sorting by user-defined parameters in a user-defined order. The user should also be able to have the system decode all abbreviations and symbols used on the record.

### 16.2.6 Export Facilities

Computerized terminology files can be used to produce glossaries, specialized vocabularies or other printed publications, provided records can be selected by subject field and subfield, and the desired fields of the record can be exported in the desired order to an intermediate file that a desktop or other electronic publishing system can process.

All terminology file management systems should provide the general features described above. Other features might be required depending on file size and type and on the anticipated use of the file.

For a translator's **personal terminology file** of fairly modest size (several thousand records), a management system for flat files is sufficient. The only processing involved consists in indexing designated fields for the purpose of querying.

A **departmental terminology file** typically contains tens of thousands of records accessed by a number of users. The software requirements here are much more stringent if such a massive quantity of information is to be managed without compromising response time. The integrity of the file must also be protected by preventing unauthorized addition, deletion, modification or copying of file contents. Management of such large files should be centralized and easily controlled. Last but not least, the software package must be able to run on a network operating system and office integration software like Microsoft Windows if networking and multiprocessing are to be possible.

## 16.3 Terminology Files and Machine-Aided Translation

The potential of computerized applications has been explored in many linguistic disciplines, including terminology. Based on research in the 1950s, machine translation systems were ambitiously developed to enable computers to translate texts. Although the results have been generally disappointing, machine translation research has spawned machine-*aided* translation (MAT) systems which can be useful for certain applications. Terminologists may wonder whether their files can be integrated with MAT dictionaries. The present state of knowledge and current techniques offer only very limited opportunity for MAT systems to use terminology files. Such programs cannot manage ambiguity. They cannot, for instance, distinguish whether an expression like *pricing model* is used as a verb phrase (He is *pricing model* airplanes) or a noun phrase (The *pricing model* needs adjustment). Direct use of terminology files by such programs could thus generate too much noise. Effectively interfacing MAT systems and terminology files is only in its infancy.

## 16.4 Machine-Aided Terminological Research

There are several prerequisites to successfully introducing the computer as a tool for terminological research. Any application failing to take this into account could be counterproductive.[2]

---

[2]. The following discussion is based on the works of P. Plante and L. Dumas, "Le dépouillement terminologique assisté par ordinateur," and P. Auger, P. Drouin and M.-C. L'Homme, "Automatisation des procédures de travail en terminographie."

Any terminologist called upon to do research by machine-aided methods must completely master all aspects of traditional methods: identifying terms, determining the constituents of complex terms, and deciding what context should be cited to bring out semantically relevant descriptors. The computer is no substitute for these basic abilities. In addition to such linguistic skills, the terminologist must have a good knowledge of the subject field or domain being researched. A terminologist working by traditional methods gradually acquires domain-specific knowledge as texts are scanned for terms. With automatic methods, this benefit is lost since, as we will see, it is the computer that scans the documents. Knowledge of the subject field must hence be gained by some other means, e.g. by reading and study. A good knowledge of the subject field is indispensable if the relevance of terminological units is to be judged, the concepts understood, and their different rendering in different languages appreciated.

### 16.4.1   Corpus Input

The use of computerized working methods requires a corpus of machine-readable texts. Texts may either be in ASCII format, e.g. files obtained from full-text documentary databases, or be put in this format after being scanned optically or keyed in manually.

Although more and more information is becoming available in the form of full-text databases, the choice of electronic publications remains very limited compared to that of printed publications. Copyright and cost are much more formidable obstacles to acquiring such database information than conversion. Optical scanning does not yet seem to be the ideal solution. It remains rather costly and is not yet sufficiently reliable, despite the fairly low error rates. The efficiency of manual input essentially depends on the skill of the word processing staff. At best, however, it is slow and costly.

Because of these difficulties, rigorous criteria must be applied in selecting a machine-readable corpus. The quality of the material on which the research is based remains much more important than the sheer quantity of text. While the computer's storage and processing capacity are large, they are not unlimited. To avoid a deluge of extraneous information, the criteria used in selecting documentation for non-computerized term research must be rigorously applied (texts representative of the subject field which are well written, not translated, by an authoritative author, taking a tutorial approach).

### 16.4.2 Machine-Aided Term Extraction

Using textual data analysis software, selected texts can be automatically scanned to produce an initial list of words. This list forms the basis of the nomenclature.

To carry out this first pass, the computer must be given a precise definition of what constitutes a word. This might be "a string of letters preceded and followed by a space" with hyphens, slashes and apostrophes considered as characters, and commas, periods, quotation marks and parentheses considered as spaces. Using this definition to scan the following sentence:

> Pontano's paper describes an input/output stage with a specially designed ping-pong buffer, his so-called "expansion buffer", which smooths out the short-duration PCM bursts.

would give the following list of words:

> #Pontano's# #paper# #describes# #an# #input/output# #stage# #with# #a# #specially# #designed# #ping-pong# #buffer# #his# #so-called# #expansion# #buffer# #which# #smooths# #out# #the# #short-duration# #PCM# #bursts#.

The output practically duplicates the scanned text and is of little interest *per se*. This is why a "stop list" of words that cannot form terminological units is generally included with the definition of a word. This list might include all pronouns, articles, prepositions, interjections, and conjunctions. Rules might be applied to eliminate all words of three or fewer letters and all words ending in -*ly*. The more words added to the stop list and, to an even larger extent, the more rules applied, the greater the risk that words that can form real terminological units will be eliminated.

The initial machine-generated word list thus produced is examined by the terminologist, who tags each word that he or she thinks could be a term or part of a term. With a stop list and rules, the shorter list might be manually tagged (*) as follows:

> Pontano's paper* describes input/output* stage* designed* ping-pong* buffer* so-called expansion* buffer* smooths* short-duration* bursts*.

Note that one of the system's rules has eliminated *PCM* and that the terminologist has retained *paper* and *designed* because they could form part of a term elsewhere in the text.

Some indexing systems give the frequency with which a word appears in the text. Such statistics provide some measure of the potential relevance of a word. Word frequency counts, however, are at best a rough measure and can be misleading. Knowledge of the subject field is the terminologist's most valuable asset at this stage.

The words tagged form a low-level nomenclature upon which complex terminological units (syntagmatic forms) are built. This step can be carried out by word-string patterns covering potential complex terms. In English, the pattern might be any two tagged words that are adjacent in the original text. From the preceding sample sentence, this would generate the following candidate terms: *input/output stage, designed ping-pong, ping-pong buffer* and *expansion buffer*. Word-string patterns are language dependent. One useful pattern in French consists of two tagged words with either *de* or *d* (from *d'*)[3] in between. This pattern would recognize such terminological units as *force de frappe* and *coup d'État*. In extended subject-field term research, this higher-level nomenclature is combined with the lower-level list to provide the entire potential nomenclature.

To select the relevant terms from the potential nomenclature, the terminologist falls back on conventional methods, building a subject-field tree and classifying each of the terminological units kept. As yet there is no machine-made method for building subject-field trees.

### 16.4.3 Context Selection

Once a tree for the subject field has been built, and the terminological units selected and classified, a key step in the term analysis process remains—selecting the context to be cited.

For each term in the nomenclature, the text analysis and indexing system provides facilities for retrieving concordances, i.e. citations attesting to usage. This is a two-step process.

The first step is to choose a mode for setting boundaries to the context. In **length-dependent mode**, the context can be defined as "any arbitrary number of lines preceding and following the line of text where the terminological unit appears." In **grammar-dependent mode**, the context can be defined as "the sentence in which the term appears," a sentence being all text falling either between two full stops or between the beginning of a paragraph and a full stop.

Each mode has its advantages and drawbacks. With length-dependent mode, the terminologist must indicate manually the exact boundaries for all cited contexts. The likelihood of losing important information, however, can be minimized

---

3. The apostrophe must be equated with a space in French, otherwise articles, negative particles, and other words, when followed by a vowel would create a deluge of spurious words, e.g. *C'est l'inondation totale, n'est-ce pas?*

by increasing the length of the surrounding text. With grammar-dependent mode, a coherent sentence is displayed. Since the sentence might not contain all the pertinent semantic features included in the text, the terminologist might need to check adjacent sentences to make sure none have been lost. The terminologist's goal during this first step is to ensure that for all meaningful contexts, the citation is coherent for the reader and includes as much semantically relevant information as possible.

During the second step in the context-selection process, the terminologist chooses the best citation for each term in the nomenclature, i.e. the citation that best illustrates the concept covered by the term.

### 16.4.4 Making Monolingual Records

The indexing system automatically generates the reference (source and page number) for the terms tagged and the citations selected. The information collected can thus be transferred or exported automatically to the appropriate fields of a terminology record (entry term, justification, source, page).

### 16.4.5 Completing Records

The resulting records are monolingual. To make bilingual or multilingual records, corresponding terms in each language must be matched by comparing the descriptors or semantic features provided by the citation(s) on each record.

Once the semantic features justifying the terminological correspondence have been found, the monolingual records are merged. The date, any usage, semantic or grammatical labels, and the field and subfield from the tree are added manually to make a complete and valid record.

## 16.5 TERMINO—A More Promising Approach

The analytical approach just described presents numerous stumbling blocks which are side-stepped to a large degree by TERMINO, a software package developed by *Centre ATO*, a centre for computerized text analysis affiliated with the *Université du Québec à Montréal*. The package does not rely on purely character- and word-string matching techniques, but applies a level of morphosyntactic analysis. Although this does not eliminate the need for the terminologist's judgment at various stages in the process, it does provide more reliable and better-filtered data. The package also better integrates context selection with the rest of the terminological research process.

Unfortunately, TERMINO currently works on French text only. Thus the software is of limited use in producing bilingual terminology records.[4]

### 16.6 A Proviso or Two

Human judgment remains a very important factor in computer-aided terminological research today. It is thus essential to ensure that the terminologist making judgments masters all requisite skills and has an adequate knowledge of the subject field under study. Of course, the matter is hardly closed. Progress in artificial intelligence could one day make it possible to identify descriptors and pair concepts in different languages automatically. Such feats are currently beyond the state of the art. It is important, however, for terminologists to stay abreast of advances in computational linguistics and information science if the profession is to benefit from and contribute to developments in these related fields.

It would also be an error to believe that the automation of terminological research will enable domain experts to establish the vocabulary for their subject field without the contribution of terminologists. Terminological research requires

---

4. For more information about TERMINO, refer to the articles by J. Perron, "Présentation du progiciel de dépouillement terminologique assisté par ordinateur : Termino," and by S. David and P. Plante, "Le progiciel Termino : de la nécessité d'une analyse morphosyntaxique pour le dépouillement terminologique des textes."

linguistic skills to isolate terms and link them with the relevant semantic features. The domain expert can certainly acquire such skills but would then have to receive the same training as a terminologist. The cooperative effort of the terminologist and the expert remains indispensable in any serious terminological research, whether machine-aided or not.

## BIBLIOGRAPHY

Ananiadou, S. "Towards a methodology for automatic term recognition." PhD thesis. University of Manchester, 1988.

Auger, Pierre, Patrick Drouin and Marie-Claude L'Homme. "Automatisation des procédures de travail en terminographie." *Meta* (special issue: "La terminologie dans le monde : orientations et recherches") 36, 1 (March 1991): 121–127.

Corbeil, Jean-Claude. "Terminologie et banques de données d'information scientifique." *Actualité terminologique*. Ottawa: Secrétariat d'État, 23 (1988): 5–6

David, Sophie and Pierre Plante. "Le progiciel Termino : de la nécessité d'une analyse morphosyntaxique pour le dépouillement terminologique des textes." In *Les Industries de la langue : perspectives des années 1990*. Montréal: Office de la langue française and Société des traducteurs du Québec, 1990, pp. 71–87.

Leonhardt, Christine. "LATTER, the terminologist's workstation." In *Proceedings from the International Symposium on Terminology and Documentation in Specialized Communication*. Ottawa: Minister of Supply and Services Canada, 1992, pp. 257–275.

Perron, Jean. "Présentation du progiciel de dépouillement terminologique assisté par ordinateur : Termino." In *Les Industries de la langue : perspectives des années 1990*. Montréal: Office de la langue française and Société des traducteurs du Québec, 1990, pp. 715–755.

Plante, Pierre and Lucie Dumas. "Le dépouillement terminologique assisté par ordinateur." *Terminogramme*. Québec : Office de la langue française, 46 (1988): 24 ff.

## EXERCISES

1. For the purpose of defining a word, should the hyphen in English be considered a letter or a space? Scan a few pages of a technical text for examples of the use of the hyphen, then discuss the advantages of and drawbacks to your choice.

2. Repeat the exercise above for a text written in French or another language. Would you make the same choice as you did for English?

# INDEX

## A

| | |
|---|---|
| Acceptability | 158 |
| Acronyms | 142 |
| Acronymy | 142 |
| Adapted borrowing | 143 |
| Adequacy | 156 |
| Adoption | 135 |
| Affixation | 138 |
| Associative context | 72 |

## B

| | |
|---|---|
| Back-formation | 144 |
| Bibliographic databases | 165 |
| Blending | 142 |
| Borrowing | 143 |
| Bound forms | 138 |

## C

| | |
|---|---|
| Causal connections | 45 |
| Characteristics | 27, 49 |
| Classification of concepts | 44, 69 |
| Classification system | 168 |
| Clipping | 137 |
| Co-occurring expressions | 70 |
| Collocation | 70 |
| Combined clipping | 137 |
| Combining | 141 |
| Comparative terminology | 85 |
| Complex terms | 5, 31, 38 |
| Composition | 137 |
| Compound adjectives | 141 |
| Compound nouns | 140 |
| Compound verbs | 140 |
| Compounding | 140 |
| Compulsory standards | 147 |
| Concept | 38, 39 |
| Construction of definitions | 113 |
| Context selection | 71, 188 |
| Contextual analysis | 6, 71 |
| Conversion | 143 |

## D

| | |
|---|---|
| Databases | 165 |
| Defining adjectives | 114 |
| Defining adverbs | 115 |
| Defining context | 71 |
| Defining nouns | 114 |
| Defining terms | 114 |
| Defining verbs | 114 |
| Definition by genus and difference | 111 |
| Degree of lexicalization | 31, 69 |
| Determinant | 67 |
| Determinatum | 67 |
| Dictionary entry | 32 |
| Direct borrowing | 143 |
| Documentation | 58, 161 |
| Documentation centre | 169 |

## E

| | |
|---|---|
| Electronic media | 166 |
| Eponymy | 136 |
| Essential characteristics | 39 |
| Essential determinants | 68 |
| Etymology | 24 |
| Evaluating documentation | 166 |
| Evaluating references | 172 |
| Expansion | 135 |
| Explanatory context | 72 |
| Export facilities | 183 |
| Extrinsic relationships | 45 |

## F

| | |
|---|---|
| Foreclipping | 137 |
| Formulating a definition | 117 |
| Free forms | 138 |
| Frequency | 155 |
| Frequency labels | 89, 125 |
| Full equivalence | 85 |

## G

| | |
|---|---|
| General administrative references | 171 |
| General language references | 170 |
| General rules of term formation | 144 |
| General technical references | 171 |
| General-language standardization | 149 |
| Generic relationship | 44 |
| Geographic labels | 89, 124 |
| Glossaries | 12 |
| Good defining practices | 115 |

## H

| | |
|---|---|
| Hierarchical relationships | 44 |
| Hindclipping | 137 |

## I

| | |
|---|---|
| Import facilities | 182 |
| Inessential determinants | 68 |
| Initialisms | 142 |
| Initializing | 142 |
| Internet | 165 |
| Intrinsic relationships | 44 |

## K

| | |
|---|---|
| Knowledge structure | 44 |

## L

| | |
|---|---|
| Lexical units | 69 |
| Lexicalization | 69 |
| Lexicographical analysis | 31 |
| Lexicographical definition | 32 |
| Lexicography | 29 |
| Lexicon | 29 |
| Libraries | 164 |
| Linguistic sign | 41 |
| Loan translation | 144 |

## M

| | |
|---|---|
| Machine-aided term extraction | 186 |
| Machine-aided terminological research | 184 |
| Machine-aided translation | 179, 184 |
| Metaphor | 135 |
| Methods of definition | 111 |
| Metonymy | 136 |
| Midclipping | 137 |
| Monolingual records | 189 |
| Monosemy | 43 |
| Morphological change | 137 |
| Motivation | 42, 156 |

## N

| | |
|---|---|
| Neologisms | 131 |
| Non-hierarchical relationships | 44, 45 |

## O

| | |
|---|---|
| Object | 38, 40 |
| Onomatopoeia | 144 |
| Operational definition | 113 |
| Oppositional relationships | 45 |
| Original-language documentation | 161 |

## P

| | |
|---|---|
| Partial equivalence | 86 |
| Phrasal compounds | 141 |
| Polysemous terms | 153 |

| | |
|---|---|
| Polysemy | 24, 42, 43 |
| Prefixes | 138 |
| Profession labels | 124 |
| Pseudo-synonyms | 121, 123, 125, 129 |

## Q

| | |
|---|---|
| Quasi-synonyms | 121, 123, 127 |
| Query facilities | 182 |

## R

| | |
|---|---|
| Real synonyms | 121, 123, 126 |
| Referent | 23 |
| Registers | 87, 88 |
| Rules of definition | 109 |

## S

| | |
|---|---|
| Scanning for terms | 60 |
| Semantic change | 135 |
| Semantic features | 27, 32, 71 |
| Semantic field | 27 |
| Semantic labels | 86 |
| Semantic range | 25 |
| Semantics | 23 |
| Semiotic triangle | 37 |
| Sign | 23 |
| Signified | 37, 41 |
| Signifier | 37, 41 |
| Simple terms | 5, 31, 38 |
| Situation | 29 |
| Situational context | 15 |
| Sociolinguistic labels | 87, 124 |
| Special-language standardization | 149 |
| Specialized documentation | 171 |
| Specialized terms | 7 |
| Standardization | 147 |
| Standards | 147 |
| Standards-writing organizations | 173 |
| Stem | 138 |
| Studies of synonyms | 125 |
| Subject-field breakdown | 60 |
| Suffixes | 139 |
| Synchronic semantics | 24 |
| Synonymous definition | 113 |
| Synonyms | 154 |
| Synonymy | 24, 42, 44 |

## T

| | |
|---|---|
| Target audience | 55 |
| Technical standards | 147 |
| Temporal labels | 89, 124 |
| Term | 38, 67 |
| Term banks | 179 |
| Term creation | 6 |
| Term formation | 131 |
| Term identification | 5 |
| Term research | 47 |
| TERMINO | 189 |
| Terminological analysis | 31, 67, 75 |
| Terminological definitions | 109 |
| Terminological phrases | 6, 38 |
| Terminological unit | 180 |
| Terminology | 3, 4 |
| Terminology banks | 165 |
| Terminology file management systems | 181 |
| Terminology files | 181 |
| Terminology files and databases | 11 |
| Terminology record | 10, 33, 179 |
| Terminology reference library | 166 |
| Terminology research oganizations | 175 |
| Terminology standardization | 150 |
| Terminology standardization process | 153 |

| | |
|---|---|
| Terminology standards | 151 |
| Terminology studies | 164 |
| Terminology unit | 38, 67, 69 |
| Terms | 3 |
| Textual correspondence | 10 |
| Textual databases | 165 |
| Textual match | 90 |
| Types of contexts | 71 |
| Typographic devices | 70 |

## U

| | |
|---|---|
| Units of discourse | 31 |
| Usability | 155 |
| Usage labels | 87 |

## V

| | |
|---|---|
| Vocabularies | 11 |
| Vocabulary | 3 |
| Voluntary standards | 147 |

## W

| | |
|---|---|
| Words | 3 |

**AGMV** Marquis
MEMBRE DE SCABRINI MEDIA
Québec, Canada
2004